Dynamic Locational Phases of Economic Activity in the Globalized World

Toshiharu Ishikawa

Dynamic Locational Phases of Economic Activity in the Globalized World

Institute of Economic Research, Chuo University
IERCU
中央大学経済研究所
1964

Springer

Toshiharu Ishikawa
Institute of Economic Research
Chuo University
Hachioji, Tokyo
Japan

ISBN 978-981-10-0523-7 ISBN 978-981-10-0524-4 (eBook)
DOI 10.1007/978-981-10-0524-4

Library of Congress Control Number: 2016932322

Printed on acid-free paper

This Springer imprint is published by SpringerNature
The registered company is Springer Science+Business Media Singapore Pte Ltd.

Preface

This book analyzes retailers' market areas, the manufacturers' factory locations, and city systems' structures in the globalized world. The activities of the retailing and manufacturing industries are crucial economic elements to build a framework for people's daily lives. These activities are concretely realized in cities and city systems. Retailers' locations and their market areas establish the basic structure of consumption activity and form the core of individual cities. Manufacturers' factories, which provide various kinds of employment for people, are located in cities because the daily lives of workers in the factories are sustained by the functions of the cities surrounding them. That is, both the consumption and production activities provide the economic base of cities while, at the same time, these activities are maintained by the city system. This book explains the retailers' market areas, the manufacturers' factory locations, and the structure of the city systems, and shows the mechanisms by which the spatial patterns of both industries—retailing and manufacturing—and the city systems are organized in a space.

In addition, the locational changes of the two industries and the structural variation of the city system are analyzed. The book clarifies the mechanisms of the locational changes of the retailing and manufacturing industries due to the growing economic globalization from the point of view of the determination of a firm's location. The book then deals with variation of the city system: After proposing a new way of construction of the city system on the basis of the market areas, it explains the mechanism of change of the city system, which is brought about by reduction of transportation costs.

This book consists of three parts. Part I shows the mechanism of the organization of the retailers' market areas and explains changes of the market areas by introducing the concept of the contact price curve for consideration. The retailers' market areas formed at one time are altered by reduction of the transportation cost per mile. The shape and size of the retailers' market areas are changed in different ways. The optimal market area shape is not confined to a hexagon; a triangle or a square can be the optimal shape for retailers in spatial competitive equilibrium. The shape that is optimal for retailers is dependent on the type of competition among retailers and the cost conditions. Also, while the market area size is shrunk by the reduction of the transportation costs per mile in some cases, the market area size is expanded in other cases. It is shown in Part I that the locational pattern of retailers varies greatly from the existing pattern which was established in a time before globalization.

Locations of the manufacturers' factories are examined in Part II of this book. In the days when production activity of firms was confined to a country or a small area, the location factors were limited to a group of general location factors, transportation costs, labor costs, and agglomeration economies. In the times of economic globalization, firms' production activities are expanding across national borders. The corporate tax rates and the interest rates of countries become important location factors; these factors are decisively important when manufacturing firms select a country to locate their factories. Part II begins its analysis by clarifying the transformation of factories' production modes in an agglomeration and shows that the fragmentation of factories' production processes are prepared from the starting point of the agglomeration formation; economic globalization gives the manufacturing firms the motivation of a spatial departure of the fragmented blocs to a location outside the agglomeration. This part of the book then proposes a search method and the concept of a "location prospective area" to the manufacturing firms. By using this method, the manufacturing firms can find a new location site of a fragmented production bloc with low search costs. The manufacturers set a locational prospective area in a large geographical area, and they select a region within the location prospective area by considering various social and economic location factors.

Part III of the book moves its focus to the city system laid out in a region. Nowadays the spatial range of retailing and manufacturing activities are spread beyond individual cities' areas. As a result, the city system and network of the city systems become an important spatial base on which economic activities of various kinds of firms are realized. Part III introduces a new theoretical way of constructing a city system, called the "flexible market area" theory. This theory explains the new formation mechanism of the city system and describes the structural change of the established city system: By using knowledge of the retailers' market areas that is analyzed in Part I, the formation of the city system and a mechanism of the change of the established city system are explained differently than in preceding analyses. Then the reciprocal relationships between the cities within a city system are examined on the basis of the analysis of land rent in the cities' areas. Finally, Part III looks into the relationships between the city systems and the social and economic performances achieved in regions using data from Japan. This examination shows that there are clear relationships between the city systems and the performances achieved in regions. The study presented in Part III shows that the city system plays a role as a location factor to attract factories from outside the region. It suggests that the theoretical results derived are useful for policy makers in existing industrialized countries to deliberate on the reformation of city systems to revitalize the regional economy.[1]

Toshiharu Ishikawa

[1]The many academic results presented in this book have been achieved through the support of the Japanese Ministry of Education, Supported Program for the Strategic Research Foundation at private Universities, 2013–2017, and the Japan Society for the Promotion of Science (Grant-in-Aid for Scientific Research (C) 26380316).

Contents

Part II Location Theory of Manufacturing Industry

Part I
Location Theory of Retailing Industry

Chapter 1
Market Areas of Retailers in Linear Space

1.1 Formation Mechanism of a Monopoly Retailer's Market

1.1.1 Basic Assumptions

In this chapter, the assumptions are set for analyzing the formation mechanism of a monopoly retailer's market in a linear space. Consumers reside on a long linear space with the same density 1, which is shown by the bottom line in Fig. 1.1a. A monopoly retailer is located at point A on the bottom line in Fig. 1.1a. All consumers have the same linear demand function, which is given by Eq. (1.1):

$$q = a - b(p + tu) \tag{1.1}$$

here, q is the quantity demanded for consumer goods, a is the maximum reservation price, t is the transportation cost per mile, p is the price of the goods, u is the distance from a consumer to the retailer, and b is the parameter (assumed to be 1 for simplicity of the analysis). The demand curve of each consumer is a linear shape, as illustrated by Fig. 1.1b. There are two reasons to use a linear demand curve: (1) the linearity is appropriate because it is expected to be the least departed from the real shape when we do not know the exact shape, and (2) assuming a linear demand function provides an opportunity to obtain tentative useful results in the early stage of the analysis.

The term (p + tu) in Eq. (1.1) represents the delivered prices of the goods to individual consumers in the linear space. The delivered prices of the goods to consumers are shown by the two upward lines, p–E and p–W, in Fig. 1.1a. Thus, each consumer's demand for the goods is indicated by the vertical height of the length from the line M–N to the downward lines q'–M or q'–N in Fig. 1.1c. For example, the consumer who resides at point d_1 in Fig. 1.1a purchases the goods by

T. Ishikawa, *Dynamic Locational Phases of Economic Activity in the Globalized World*, DOI 10.1007/978-981-10-0524-4_1

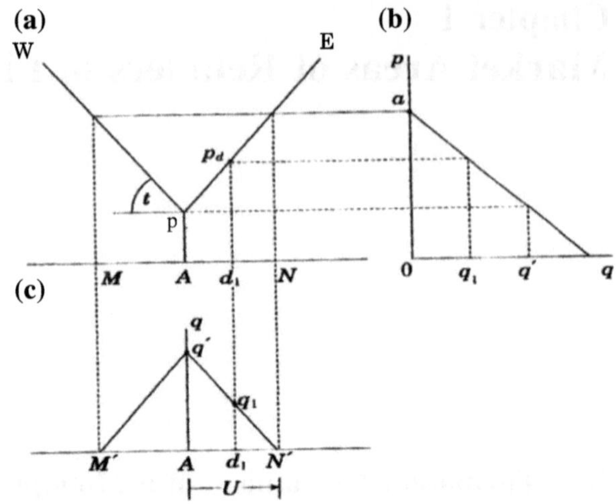

Fig. 1.1 Formation of the market in a linear space

0–q_1 in Fig. 1.1b according to the delivered price p_d, which is shown in Fig. 1.1a. The quantity 0–q_1 is transferred to the vertical line d_1–q_1 in Fig. 1.1c.

The retailer has a linear cost function, as given by Eq. (1.2):

$$C = kQ + F \tag{1.2}$$

here, C is the total cost; k and F are the marginal and fixed costs, respectively; and Q denotes the retailer's sales amount.

1.1.2 Formation of the Market Area and Derivation of the Retailer's Profit

Suppose that the retailer sells goods at price p to consumers on the linear space. Consumers for whom the delivered price of the goods is less than the maximum reservation price a purchase the goods according to the demand function. The quantity demand for the goods becomes zero for the consumers who reside at the points where the delivered price reaches the maximum reservation price a. The two points are shown by M and N in Fig. 1.1a. The distance from the consumer whose demand for the goods is just zero to the retailer is denoted by U. Using Eq. (1.3a) the distance U is given by Eq. (1.3b).

$$Q = a - p - tU = 0 \tag{1.3a}$$

$$U = (a - p)/t \tag{1.3b}$$

Fig. 1.2 Relationship between price and sales quantity in a linear market

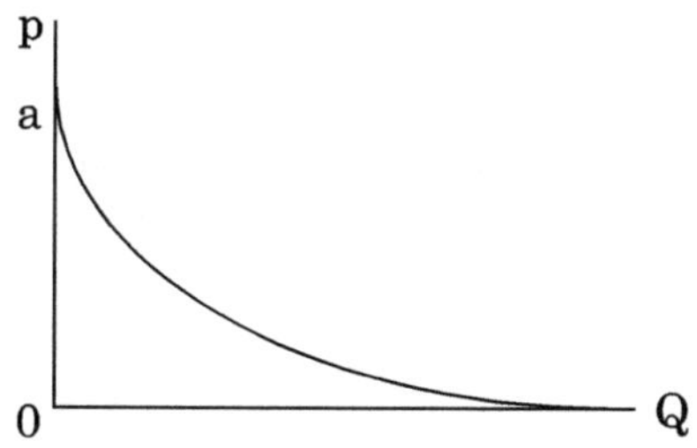

The retailer's market length $2U$ is given by $2(a - p)/t$. Demand for the goods of individual consumers is shown in Fig. 1.1b. For instance, as mentioned above, the demand of the consumer at point d_1 is indicated by the length of the line d_1–q_1.

The retailer's sales quantity Q is given by the area of the triangle formed by points M'–q'–N' in Fig. 1.1c. The sales quantity is also obtained by Eq. (1.4a). Because the market size U is a function of the price of goods, the sales quantity is given by Eq. (1.4b). Figure 1.2 shows the relationship between the price of goods and the sales amount.

$$Q = 2\int_0^U (a - p - tu)\mathrm{d}u \tag{1.4a}$$

$$= (a - p)^2/t \tag{1.4b}$$

The retailer's revenue is obtained by Eq. (1.5). The line of 0–R^*–a in Fig. 1.3 illustrates the relationship between the revenue and the price:

Fig. 1.3 Retailer's revenue and cost curve in a linear market

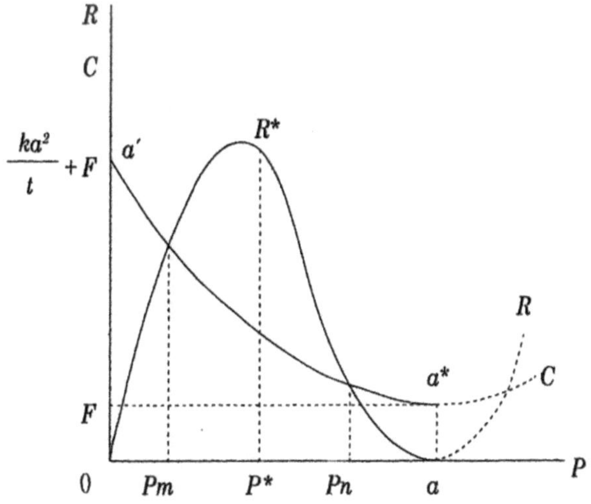

$$R = p(a-p)^2/t \tag{1.5}$$

The retailer's cost is derived as Eq. (1.6) by using Eqs. (1.2) and (1.4b). The retailer's cost is shown by the line of a'–$a*$ in Fig. 1.3. The value of point a' in Fig. 1.3 is $(ka^2/t + F)$.

$$C = (k/t)(a-p)^2 + F \tag{1.6}$$

From Eqs. (1.5) and (1.6), the retailer's profit is derived as Eq. (1.7), which is shown by Y_0–Y' in Fig. 1.4.

$$Y = (a-p)^2(p-k)/t - F \tag{1.7}$$

Optimal price $P*$ is derived by differentiating Eq. (1.7) with respect to p as Eq. (1.8):

$$P^* = (a+2k)/3 \tag{1.8}$$

Then, the optimal market length of the retailer ($2U^*$) is given as Eq. (1.9) by substituting p in Eq. (1.3b) with Eq. (1.8).

$$2U^* = 2(2/3t)(a-k) \tag{1.9}$$

As shown by Fig. 1.4, the lower bound and the upper bound of the feasible pricing range are shown by two points P_m and P_n, at which the retailer's profit becomes just zero. The corresponding market length of the lower bound and the upper bound are shown as points M_i–N_i ($I = n, m$) in Fig. 1.5. The optimal market size is given by the length limited by points $M*$ and $N*$.

It is noteworthy that at the end points of the market area of the retailer, the consumer's demand for the goods always becomes zero. Hence, the minimum

Fig. 1.4 Retailer's profit in a linear space

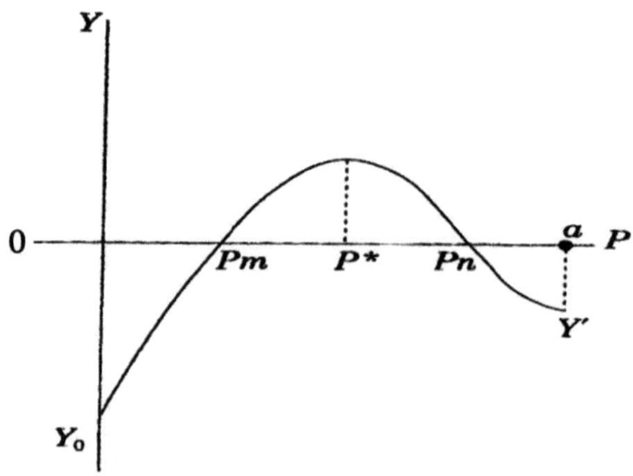

Fig. 1.5 Three market sizes of retailers

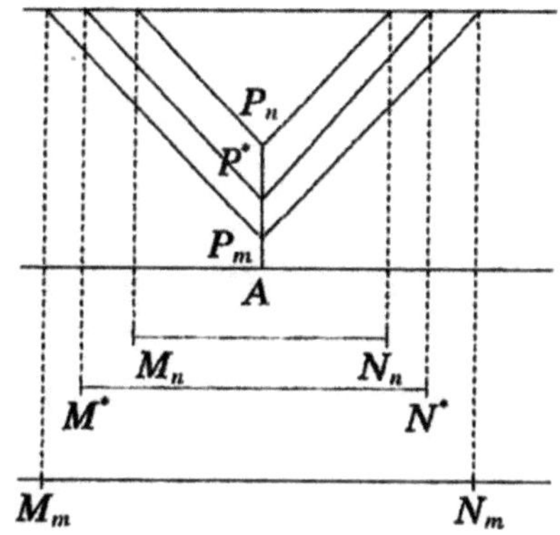

market size of the monopoly retailer is usually different from the minimum market area of the retailers under the competitive equilibrium. The minimum market size of the monopoly retailer is much larger than that of retailers under competitive equilibrium.

1.1.3 *Retailer's Price and Location in Limited Liner Space*

This section analyzes the retailer's location and the price of the goods in a limited linear space. When the space is limited to a certain length, the retailer's location becomes an important issue. Suppose that the retailer is given a limited linear space, which is the length segmented by points M and N in Fig. 1.6a; the retailer's location is denoted by x, which is the distance from the end point M to the retailer. In this case, the retailer's sales quantity is obtained by Eq. (1.10). The sales quantity is shown by the area shaped by points N–M–M'–q'–N' in Fig. 1.6c.

$$Q = \int_0^x (a - p - tu)\mathrm{d}u + \int_0^{L-x} (a - p - tu)\mathrm{d}u \tag{1.10}$$

The retailer's profit is given by Eq. (1.11):

$$Y = (p - k)(a - p - tx/2)x + (a - p - t(L - x)/2)(L - x) - F \tag{1.11}$$

Differentiating Eq. (1.11) by x gives the optimal retailer's location as Eq. (1.12):

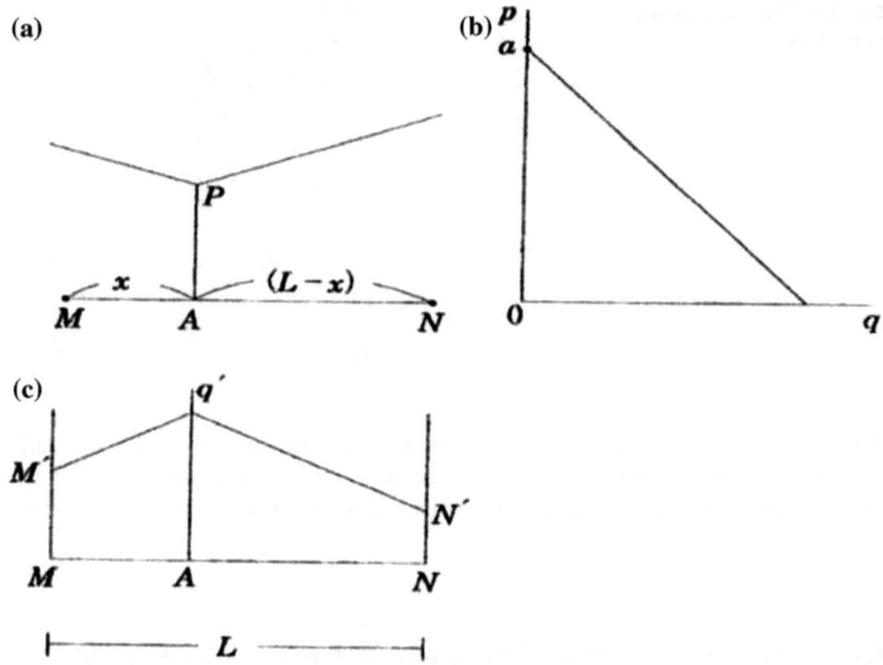

Fig. 1.6 Retailer's price and sales quantity in a limited market

$$X^* = L/2 \tag{1.12}$$

The optimal location is determined at the midpoint of the limited linear space. The profit function of the retailer is derived as Eq. (1.13). The optimal price of retailer P^* is obtained as Eq. (1.14).

$$Y = (p - k)(2(a - p - tL/2)(L/2)) - F \tag{1.13}$$

$$P^* = (a + k)/2 - tL/8 \tag{1.14}$$

Equation (1.14) shows that if the retailer's market is limited to a certain length, the retailer's optimal price is influenced by the transportation cost per mile and the given market length.

1.2 Emergence of Competition and Competition Styles

1.2.1 Retailers' Situation Before the Emergence of Free-Entry Competition

Assume that retailers can enter a linear market space as far as the retailer's profit is not negative and that the transportation cost per mile is the highest level at which each retailer achieves the just zero profit with the optimal price and the optimal market length. In this case, as shown by the bold lines in Fig. 1.7, the retailers' locations are indicated by A_i ($i = 0, 1, 2$) and their market length is $(4/3t)$ $(a - k)$, which is shown by the distance between points m_0 and m_1; their price is shown by P^*. All delivered prices to all consumers are indicated by the bold upward oblique lines in Fig. 1.7. This situation is described that although there are many retailers exist in the linear market space, each retailer's price and market are the same as those of the monopoly retailer, and there is no competition between the retailers because the transportation cost is too high to compete between them. It is considered that the situation depicted by the bold lines in Fig. 1.7 illustrates the state of the retailers in the linear market space before the competition begins in the retailing industry.

1.2.2 Change of Retailers' Situation Due to a Reduction of Transportation Costs

Let us suppose that the transportation cost per mile is reduced in the situation described in Fig. 1.7; by the reduction of the transportation cost, the delivered price to each consumer is decreased, which is indicated by the dotted lines in Fig. 1.7. Because the optimal price of each retailer is not affected by the reduction of the transportation cost, the optimal price remains at the same level and the market size of the retailers is not changed. The delivered price at boundary points decreases from a to p', which is hereafter referred to as the *contact price* (*CP*) in this analysis.

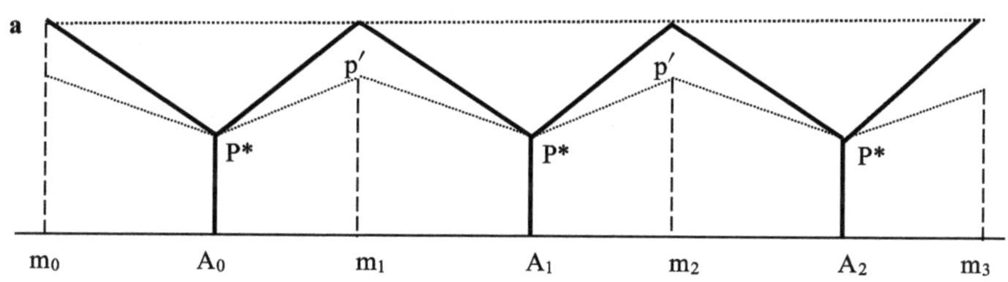

Fig. 1.7 State of retailers before and after competition and emergence of the contact price

It is thus said that each retailer's market size is dictated by the CP and that the pressure of the competition between the retailers is revealed by the level of the CP.

Now, due to a reduction of the transportation costs, each retailer obtains positive profit with the same market size. The positive profits give rise to the competition in the retail industry. Because the optimal market length is larger than that dictated by the CP, the existing retailers have a motive to expand their market size. Potential retailers seek entry to this market. The reduction of the transportation cost generates the competition between the retailers and starts to alter the retail market structure established in the early stage of economic development.

1.2.3 Analysis of Competition Styles Between the Retailers

This section analyzes the effects of a reduction of the transportation cost per mile on the retailers' markets and explains the mechanism of the reduction to change the retailers' market size and the price of the goods.

When the linear market space is opened to potential retailers and the transport cost is adequately low, the competition among the retailers begins and a free-entry competitive equilibrium is established in the market space. In a free-entry equilibrium, two conditions must be satisfied: (1) each retailer sets the price that maximizes the retailer's profit. This condition is indicated by Eq. (1.15); and (2) each retailer's profit is just zero. Equation (1.16) shows the second condition:

$$\mathrm{d}Y/\mathrm{d}p = (p-k)(\mathrm{d}Q/\mathrm{d}p + \mathrm{d}Q/\mathrm{d}U \cdot \mathrm{d}U/\mathrm{d}p) + Q = 0 \tag{1.15}$$

$$Y = (p-k)Q - F = 0 \tag{1.16}$$

Solving the above simultaneous equations system with respect to p and U gives a competitive equilibrium price p^* and an equilibrium market size U^*, which is the half of the equilibrium market length. The value of the term $\mathrm{d}U/\mathrm{d}p$ in Eq. (1.15) depends on Eq. (1.17):

$$\mathrm{d}U/\mathrm{d}p = (\mathrm{d}p'/\mathrm{d}p - 1)/2t, \tag{1.17}$$

where p' is the price of the retailer, which is located next to the retailer in question. The term $\mathrm{d}p'/\mathrm{d}p$ in Eq. (1.17) is called the *conjectural variation of price* (CVP) by the retailer in question. When the CVP is 1, the competition style is Lösch competition. When the CVP is 0, the competition style is Hotelling–Smithies (H–S). Lastly, when the CVP is −1, the competition style is Greenhut–Ohta (G–O). These

Table 1.1 Equilibrium market situations in the three different competition styles

	Lösch		H–S		G–O	
t	*p*	*U*	*p*	*U*	*p*	*U*
1.437	0.34	0.45	0.34	0.45	0.34	0.45
1.4	0.37	0.39	0.35	0.39	0.33	0.4
1.2	0.41	0.31	0.35	0.32	0.3	0.35
1.1	0.43	0.29	0.34	0.31	0.29	0.34
1	0.44	0.28	0.33	0.3	0.27	0.34
0.9	0.45	0.26	0.32	0.3	0.26	0.35
0.8	0.45	0.25	0.3	0.29	0.24	0.35
0.6	0.47	0.24	0.27	0.3	0.2	0.38
0.4	0.48	0.22	0.22	0.33	0.16	0.43
0.2	0.49	0.21	0.16	*0.43*	0.12	*0.57*

three styles are typical competition modes between the retailers.[1] Thus, the next section analyzes the three different equilibria that result from the three kinds of the competition styles among the retailers.

1.3 Equilibrium Price and Market Size Established in Linear Markets

1.3.1 Equilibrium Prices and Market Sizes in Three Different Competition Styles

Let us assign the numerical values of parameters in Eqs. (1.15) and (1.16); $a = 1$, $F = 0.1$, and $k = 0.01$. The transport cost per mile t is assumed to be ten different values in the range from 1.437, which is the highest level, to 0.2. The above two equation systems were solved with respect to p and U against each transportation cost per mile. The equilibrium values obtained in the three different kinds of competition styles are indicated in Table 1.1.

As shown in Table 1.1, when the linear market space is under the Lösch competition type, the retailer's price simply increases and the market length shrinks according to the decreasing transportation cost. Under the G–O competition type (G–O), the retailer's price simply decreases, while the market length shrinks when the transportation cost is in the high range; it turns to expand as the transportation cost decreases. When the transport cost is 0.2, the retailers' market length is larger

[1]The concept of the conjectural price variation is clearly introduced into spatial competition by Capozza-Van Order (1978). The works of Hotelling (1929), Lerner and Singer (1937), Smithies (1941), Greenhut and Ohta (1973), and Schöler (1993) contribute to the understanding of this concept. By introducing this concept into consideration, the analysis of the firms' location and the market area in spatial free-entry competitive equilibria has been greatly developed (Ishikawa and Toda 1995).

than the original size. When the market space is under the Hotelling–Smithies competition type (H–S), the equilibrium values show the complicated changes: the retailer's price increases until the transportation cost decreases to 1.4 and decreases as the transportation cost is reduced; the retailers' market length shrinks until the transport cost decreases to 1, and the market length expands as the transportation cost reduces. It is very interesting that the equilibrium market situation largely changes according to the competition style between the retailers in the market space.

1.3.2 The Mechanisms of a Changing Equilibrium by Competition Style

There seems to be no commonality between the changes of the retailers' equilibrium situations in the three competition styles according to the reducing transportation cost. Checking the CP, however, gives the commonality between the changes of the three equilibrium situations. Table 1.2 shows the CPs of the equilibrium situations derived from the three different kinds of competition styles. As the transportation cost decreases, all of the CPs established in the three competition styles become lower. Hence, it can be concluded that a reduction of the transportation cost per mile affects the equilibrium values in order to lower the CP, irrespective of the competition styles. In other words, when the transportation cost decreases, the retailers change the price and market length to reduce the CP regardless of the competition styles.

The reason that the price and market length in competitive equilibrium change in different directions according to the reduction of the transportation cost can be explained as follows. There are three ways to reduce the CP. The first way is to reduce the price at the retailer's store and to shorten the distance between the retailer and its market boundary due to the reduction of the transportation cost per mile. The second way is to reduce the transportation costs by the decreasing the

Table 1.2 Decrease of the contact price

	Lösch	H–S	G–O
t	CP	CP	CP
1.437	0.98665	0.98665	0.98665
1.4	0.916	0.916	0.89
1.2	0.782	0.794	0.72
1.1	0.749	0.771	0.664
1	0.72	0.74	0.61
0.9	0.684	0.72	0.575
0.8	0.65	0.682	0.52
0.6	0.614	0.65	0.428
0.4	0.568	0.612	0.332
0.2	0.532	0.576	0.234

distance between the retailer and its market boundary. This way implies that the reduction of the CP by the decreasing the distance is larger than the increase of the CP by increasing the price at the stores of the retailers. The third way is to decrease the price at the retailer's store by utilizing the scale economies, which are derived by enlarging its market area size. It also leads to a reduction of the CP because the reduction of the CP by the decreasing the price is larger than the effect by the increasing the distance.

When the market space is under a Lösch competition style, the retailers take only the second way because the decrease of the transportation cost obtained by the decreasing the distance is larger than the increase of the price at the stores of the retailers; consequently, the CP is reduced. When the market space is under the H–S competition style and the transportation cost is relatively high, the retailers change the price and the market length like the Lösch style in order to reduce the CP. As the transportation cost per mile decreases, the retailers take the first way initially; then, they take the third way to reduce the CP. If the market space is under the Greenhut–Ohta competition style, the retailers take the first way in the relatively high transportation cost. In the relatively low transportation cost per mile, the retailers take the third way; they expand the market length to utilize the scale economies by enlarging the market area in order to reduce the CP.

1.3.3 Characteristics of the Established Market Situations

If the Lösch competition style prevails in the retail market space, the retailers' market length becomes smaller as the transportation cost decreases. Thus, it is said that because the necessary market size that is needed for new retailers to enter the market space becomes smaller and smaller, the Lösch competition style can be considered as the competition style to invite new retailers to the retail market. This competition style could correspond to the competition among the convenience stores in the real world. The G–O competition style can be considered as the style to expel some existing retailers from the retail market because the retailers' market length becomes larger beyond the original size as the transportation cost decreases. This competition style could explain the competition between large department stores in the real world. The H–S competition style is considered as the style to maintain the status quo prevailed in the market. This could correspond to the competition between supermarket stores.

The G–O competition style is the harshest for the retail industry because it tends to expel some existing rivals. The Lösch competition style is not difficult for retailers because it does not expel competitors but invites rivals outside. From the viewpoint of the consumers, the consumers' evaluation about competition styles is not the same. In the Lösch competition style, the price of goods is higher, while it shortens the distance to the retailer. In the G–O style, the price of the goods at the retailers' stores is lower, but the distance to the retailer becomes longer.

Chapter 2
Market Areas of Retailers in Plane Space

This chapter examines the retailers' market areas and prices in a plane space. Assuming two retailers in a market space, the chapter first derives the shape of the boundary between the retailers' market areas. Second, relaxing the assumption for new retailers to enter the plane market space until every retailer's profit becomes zero, the retailers' market areas and prices are established in a free-entry competitive market space.

2.1 Shapes of Boundary Between Two Retailers' Market Areas

Assume that there are only two retailers, A and B, in a plane market space and consumers reside evenly on the market space. The same kind of goods are sold by the two retailers; each consumer purchases the goods at a retailer that offers the lowest delivered price to the consumer. The sites at which the delivered prices of the two retailers become the same form the market area boundary. This subsection explains the shapes of the market boundary, which vary according to the retailers' conditions.

2.1.1 Derivation of the Shapes of Market Boundaries by Using Two Regular Cone Surfaces

The situations of the two retailers A and B on a plane space are shown in Fig. 2.1a. Retailer A is located at origin O on the x-y plane space. Retailer B is located at point L away from retailer A along the x axis. The price of the good at each retailer's store is shown by p_A and p_B, respectively.

T. Ishikawa, *Dynamic Locational Phases of Economic Activity in the Globalized World*, DOI 10.1007/978-981-10-0524-4_2

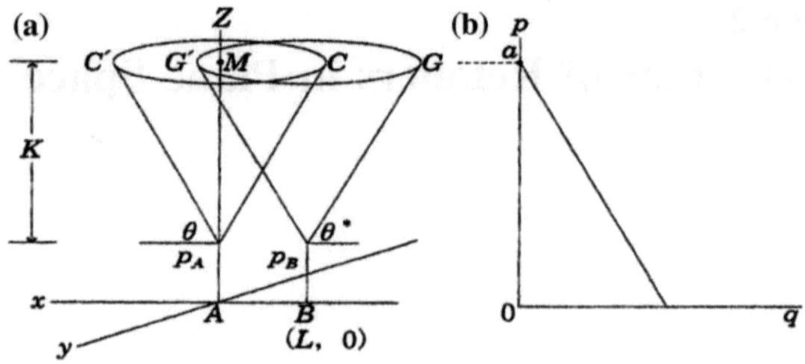

Fig. 2.1 Derivation of the market boundary by two regular cone surfaces. **a** Two regular cone surfaces, **b** Demand curve

The demand function of every consumer is given by Eq. (2.1), which is shown in Fig. 2.1b:

$$q_i = a - p_i - t_i u \quad (i = A, B) \tag{2.1}$$

Here, t_i ($i = A, B$) shows the transportation cost per mile for the retailers, A and B. The transportation costs per mile are described by θ, θ^* in Fig. 2.1a. The delivered prices of the goods are measured by the z axis in Fig. 2.1a. Thus, the level of the delivered price of retailer A to each consumer is shown by the left regular cone surface, p_ACMC. The delivered price of retailer B is indicated by the right regular cone surface, p_BGMG′. The market boundary by the two retailers' market areas is formed by the intersection of these two cone surfaces.[1]

Let us derive the market boundary shape by formulating the two cone surfaces. The height of the cone of retailer A is noted by K, as shown in Fig. 2.1a. The difference between the heights of the two cones is noted by S. For simplicity, the bottom of retailer A's cone is assumed at the origin (0, 0, 0) on the three-dimensional space. The regular cone surface of retailer A is shown by Eq. (2.2):

$$K^2\left(x^2 + y^2\right) = z^2 C^2 \tag{2.2}$$

where C is the radius of the circular market area of the retailer A. Because $K/C = \tan\theta$, Eq. (2.2) is transformed to Eq. (2.2a).

$$\left(x^2 + y^2\right)\tan^2\theta = z^2 \tag{2.2a}$$

[1]This method was introduced by Miyasaka (1970) into the market boundary analysis. He derived boundary shapes of two market areas by using two regular cone surfaces shown in Fig. 2.1a. Parr (1995) explained the market borders in a different way from that of this chapter.

In a similar way, the regular cone surface of retailer B is given by Eq. (2.3):

$$\left((x-L)^2+y^2\right)\tan^2\theta^* = (z-S)^2 \tag{2.3}$$

Hence, the market boundary of the two retailers' market areas can be determined by solving the simultaneous Eqs. (2.2a) and (2.3) by x and y. Next, subsections explain the shapes of the market area boundary according to the retailers' conditions.

2.1.2 *Boundary Shape in the Case of the Same Prices and Transportation Costs*

It is supposed that the two retailers' prices and transportation costs per mile are the same. In this case, the value of S, which indicates the difference between the prices of the retailers, is zero. Thus, solving the simultaneous Eqs. (2.2a) and (2.3) with respect to x and y gives Eq. (2.4):

$$2xL\tan^2\theta - L^2\tan^2\theta = 0 \tag{2.4}$$

Here, x is derived as $(L/2)$. The market area boundary is shown as a straight line that divides the line combining the two retailers. This boundary is shown by $b_1 - b_2$ in Fig. 2.2a.

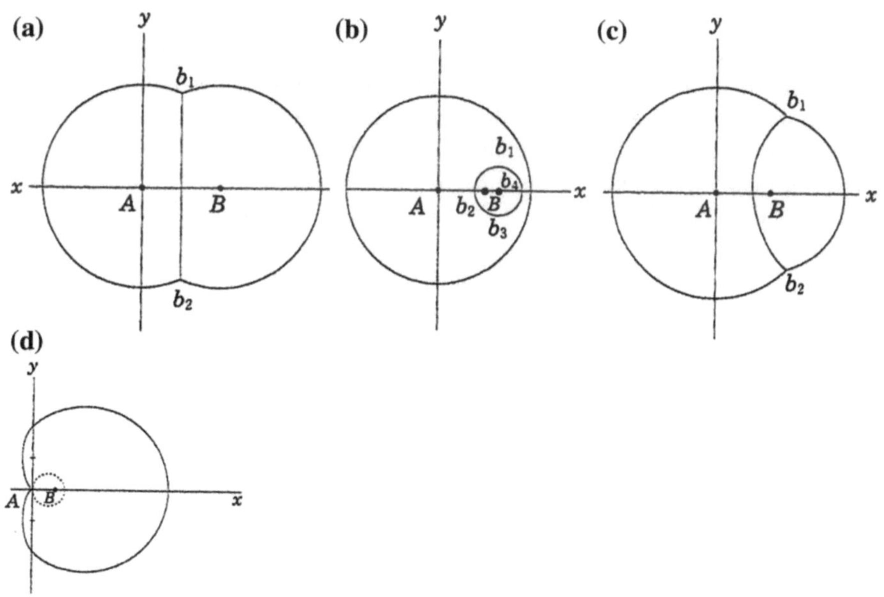

Fig. 2.2 Four shapes of the market boundary of two market areas. **a** Straight line, **b** Circle, **c** Hyperbola, **d** Limacon

2.1.3 Boundary Shape in a Case of the Same Prices and Different Transport Costs

In the second case, it is assumed that the prices at the two retailers' stores are the same, while the transportation cost per mile of retailer A is lower than that of retailer B, $\theta < \theta^*$, and $S = 0$. Solving the simultaneous Eq. (2.2a) and (2.3) gives Eq. (2.5):

$$\left(\tan^2\theta^* - \tan^2\theta\right)x^2 + \left(\tan^2\theta^* - \tan\theta\right)y^2 - 2L\tan^2\theta^* x + L^2\tan^2\theta^* = 0 \quad (2.5)$$

Let us clarify the shape indicated by the Eq. (2.5). Dividing Eq. (2.5) by $(\tan^2\theta^* - \tan^2\theta)$ gives Eq. (2.6):

$$x^2 + y^2 - 2L\tan^2\theta^* x / \left(\tan^2\theta^* - \tan^2\theta\right) + L^2\tan^2\theta^* / \left(\tan^2\theta^* - \tan^2\theta\right) = 0 \quad (2.6)$$

Equation (2.6) describes the circle of origin located at point $(L\tan^2\theta^*/(\tan^2\theta^* - \tan^2\theta), 0)$; the radius of the circle is $(L\tan^2\theta^*/(\tan^2\theta^* - \tan^2\theta))^{0.5}$. This circular market boundary is illustrated by the small circle shown by point b_1–b_2–b_3 in Fig. 2.2b, and its origin is indicated by point b_4 in Fig. 2.2b.

2.1.4 Boundary Shape in a Case of Different Prices and the Same Transportation Costs

In the third case, it is supposed that the price of the goods at retailer B's store is higher than that of retailer A by S. The transportation cost per mile is the same between the two retailers. Because the transportation cost per mile is the same, the transportation costs of the two retailers are noted by the same notation, θ. The market boundary in this case is obtained as follows. The righthand side of Eq. (2.3) is developed to Eq. (2.7):

$$\left((x - L)^2 + y^2\right)\tan^2\theta = z^2 - 2zS + S^2 \quad (2.7)$$

Substituting z in Eq. (2.7) with Eq. (2.2a) gives Eq. (2.8):

$$\left((x - L)^2 + y^2 - (x^2 + y^2)\right)\tan^2\theta - S^2 = -2zS \quad (2.8)$$

As both sides of Eq. (2.8) are squared, Eq. (2.9) is obtained:

$$\left(\left((x - L)^2 + y^2 - (x^2 + y^2)\right)\tan^2\theta - S^2\right)^2 = 4z^2S^2 \quad (2.9)$$

Substituting z^2 in Eq. (2.7) with Eq. (2.2a), then dividing it by $(1/\cot^2\theta)^2$, gives Eq. (2.10):

$$\left(L^2 - 2\mathrm{Lx} - S^2\cot^2\theta\right)^2 = 4S^2\left(x^2 + y^2\right)\cot^2\theta \tag{2.10}$$

Equation (2.10) is transformed to Eq. (2.11):

$$\left(L^2 - S^2\cot^2\theta\right)x^2 - S^2\cot^2\theta y^2 - L\left(L^2 - S^2\cot^2\theta\right)x + (1/4)\left(L^2 - S^2\cot^2\theta\right)^2 = 0 \tag{2.11}$$

Transforming the *x-y* coordination, Eq. (2.11) is shown by Eq. (2.12), which implies a hyperbola:

$$x^2/(S\cot\theta/2)^2 - y^2/\left(\left(L^2 - S^2\cot^2\theta\right)^{0.5}/2\right)^2 = 1 \tag{2.12}$$

The asymptotic lines of the hyperbola are given by Eqs. (2.13) and (2.14):

$$y = +\left(\left(L^2 - S^2\cot^2\theta\right)^{0.5}/S\cot\theta\right)x \tag{2.13}$$

$$y = -\left(\left(L^2 - S^2\cot^2\theta\right)^{0.5}/S\cot\theta\right)x \tag{2.14}$$

The boundary of the retailers' market areas in this case is shown by b_1–b_2 in Fig. 2.2c.

2.1.5 Boundary Shape in a Case of Different Prices and Different Transportation Costs

The fourth case deals with a rather complicated situation that the transportation cost per mile of retailer B is higher than that of retailer A, and the price of retailer B is lower than that of retailer A by *S*. Then, retailer B's delivered price at the location of retailer A is just equal to the price at retailer A. Retailer B's regular cone surface is indicated by Eq. (2.15):

$$\left((x - L)^2 + y^2\right)\tan\theta^* = (z + S)^2 \tag{2.15}$$

The market boundary can be obtained by solving the simultaneous Eqs. (2.2a) and (2.15) with respect to *x* and *y*. By developing the right-hand side and then substituting z^2 with Eqs. (2.2a) and (2.16) is derived:

$$\left((x-L)^2+y^2\right)\tan^2\theta^* = (x^2+y^2)\tan^2\theta + 2zS + S^2 \tag{2.16}$$

Equation (2.16) is transformed to Eq. (2.17):

$$\left(\tan^2\theta^* - \tan^2\theta\right)x^2 + \left(\tan^2\theta^* - \tan^2\theta\right)y^2 - 2\text{L}\tan^2\theta^* x + L^2\tan^2\theta^* - S^2 = 2z\text{S} \tag{2.17}$$

By squaring the both sides of Eq. (2.17) and substituting z with Eq. (2.2a), Eq. (2.18) is obtained:

$$\left(W\left(x^2+y^2\right)^2\tan^2\theta^* Lx + \tan^2\theta L^2 - S^2\right)^2 = 4S^2\tan^2\theta\left(x^2+y^2\right) \tag{2.18}$$

where $W = \tan^2\theta^* - \tan^2\theta$. Because $\tan\theta^* = S/L$, Eq. (2.18) is transformed as Eq. (2.19):

$$\left(x^2+y^2 - 2\tan^2\theta^* Lx/W\right)^2 = (2S\tan\theta/W)^2\left(x^2+y^2\right) \tag{2.19}$$

Equation (2.19) describes the limaçon, which is shown in Fig. 2.2d.

2.1.6 Boundary in a Case of the Same Retailers' Locations and Different Transportation Costs

The fifth case examines the market boundary when the prices at the stores of the two retailers are different and the transportation costs per mile also are different between the two retailers, while the location of the stores of the retailers are coincidence. In this case, the regular cone surface of retailer B is given by Eq. (2.20):

$$\left(x^2+y^2\right)\tan^2\theta^* = (z+S)^2 \tag{2.20}$$

The shape of the market boundary in this situation is derived from Eq. (2.21), which is derived by using Eqs. (2.2a) and (2.20):

$$\left(\tan^2\theta^* - \tan\theta\right)\left(x^2+y^2\right)^2 + 2S^2\left(\tan^2\theta^* + \tan^2\theta\right)\left(x^2+y^2\right) + S^4 = 0 \tag{2.21}$$

By transforming Eqs. (2.21) and (2.22) is obtained:

$$x^2+y^2 = \left(S\left(\tan^2\theta^* + \tan^2\theta\right)/\left(\tan^2\theta^* - \tan^2\theta\right)\right)^2 \tag{2.22}$$

Equation (2.22) indicates a circle with an origin located at the origin (0, 0); the radius of the circle is $S(\tan^2\theta^* + \tan^2\theta)/(\tan^2\theta^* - \tan^2\theta)$.

2.1.7 *Market Boundary Shapes Derived by a Method of Numerical Calculation*

When the two retailers' locations, prices, and transportation costs per mile are different, the shape of the market area boundary can be usually derived by using a numerical calculation. In this subsection, the following two typical market conditions are selected and the resulting market area boundaries are shown by assigning numerical values to the transport costs per mile and the retailers' prices:

(I) Retailer B's price is lower than that of retailer A and the transportation cost per mile of retailer B is higher than retailer A. Retailer B's location is moved from the origin point to the end-point of the market area of retailer A along the x axis.

(II) Retailer B's price is higher than that of retailer A and the transportation cost per mile of retailer B is higher than retailer A. Retailer B's location is moved from a point at which retailer B starts to sell its goods in the market space to the end-point of the market area of the retailer A along the x axis.

First, let us examine the market area boundary of case (I), where $\theta = 1$, $\theta^* = 1.5$ and $p_A = 5$, $p_B = 2$ are assumed. In this case, as retailer B's location is moved from the origin point of the plane to the end-point of retailer A's market area, the market area boundary is changed as shown by the curves in Fig. 2.3a; from a circle to the limaçon, and then one of the vertically stretched curves of the ellipse finally.

In case (II) where $\theta = 1$, $\theta^* = 1.5$ and $p_A = 5$, $p_B = 6$ are assumed. The location of retailer B is assumed to be moved from a point at which retailer B start to sell its goods in the market space to the end-point of the market area of the retailer A along the x axis. In this case, as retailer B's location is moved toward the end point, the market area boundary is illustrated by the curves in Fig. 2.3b. Each market boundary belongs to one of the horizontally stretched ellipse families.

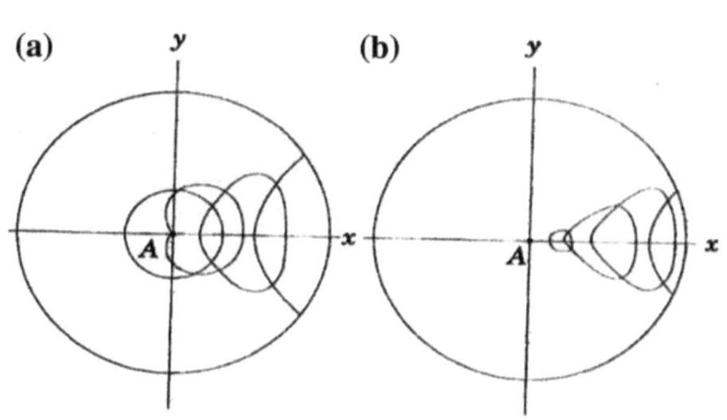

Fig. 2.3 Market boundary described by the fourth degree functions. **a** Vertically stretched ellipe curves, **b** Horizontally stretched curves

2.1.8 *A Comment on the Market Boundary Analysis*

Although the history of the analysis of the retailers' market boundary is rather long, the achievements of the analysis have not been effectively utilized. One of the reasons why the shape analysis of the market area boundary has not been successfully developed in economics is that the analysis relies on only a single method of the equation treatment: There are many complicated shapes among the market area borders so that the shapes of the market areas of the retailers are diversified. It is thus difficult to derive the sales volumes of the retailers in their market areas. If it is difficult to derive the sales volume, which is indispensable to obtain the retailers' profits and costs, the motive and incentive to analyze the market area boundaries are so weak that the significance of the market area boundary analysis is not noticed by many researchers and expert regional policy makers. It may be important to use a numerical calculation method, such as Monte Carlo, as well as equation treatment in order to grasp the sales quantity in the complicated market areas of the retailers.[2] If it would be easy to derive the sale quantities in many complicated market areas, it would stimulate the analysis of the regional economics, especially the analysis of the city systems in regions, which are the basic spatial unit of the regional economy.

2.2 Market Area in Spatial Free-Entry Equilibrium

Assuming that a plane market space is opened to allow for a new retailer to enter and the market space is under free-entry competition, this section analyses the retailers' market area sizes and market area shapes in a free-entry competitive equilibrium. Also, the prices and the delivered prices of goods established in the competitive market space are examined.

2.2.1 *Feasible Market Shapes in a Free-Entry Equilibrium*

Let us derive the potential market area shapes that can emerge in a free-entry competitive equilibrium in a market space. Assume that the same regular polynomial markets of the retailers cover a plane space and the regular polynomial markets have n apexes, and m apexes gather at an apex of the polynomial market. In this case, the vertical angle of the regular market area with n apexes is shown by $\pi(n - 2)/n$. Therefore, the condition that the vertical angle multiplied by m times makes 2π is given by $m(1 - 2/n) = 2$. Hence, the following relationship is obtained:

---

[2]The derivation of sales volumes using Monte Carlo has been conducted by Ishikawa and Toda (2002). It is applied to a retailer's location strategy in a plane space.

$$mn = 2m + 2n \tag{2.23}$$

Adding 4 to the both sides of Eq. (2.23) gives Eq. (2.24).

$$(m-2)(n-2) = 4 \tag{2.24}$$

The integer solutions of Eq. (2.24) are confined to the following the three sets:

$$(m, n) = (4, 4), (3, 6), (6, 3) \tag{2.24a}$$

The above integer solution sets mean that the shapes of market areas in a free-entry equilibrium are limited to the three shapes; square, regular triangle, and regular hexagon.

2.2.2 Market Shapes of Retailers in Free-Entry Competitive Equilibria

This subsection deals with the retailers' market area shape, which appears in a free-entry competitive equilibrium.[3] In this analysis, the same framework is used as in the preceding analysis in the linear market space. Thus, the demand function and cost function are the same those used in the analysis in the linear space. There are two conditions that must be satisfied in a free-entry competitive equilibrium: (1) each retailer's profit is just zero and (2) each retailer sets the price to maximize its profit. The two equilibrium conditions are represented by Eqs. (2.25) and (2.26), respectively:

$$Y = (p-k)Q - F = 0 \tag{2.25}$$

$$\mathrm{d}Y/\mathrm{d}p = (p-k)(\mathrm{d}Q/\mathrm{d}p + \mathrm{d}Q/\mathrm{d}U \cdot \mathrm{d}U/\mathrm{d}p) + Q = 0 \tag{2.26}$$

The term dU/dp in Eq. (2.26) is dependent on the conjectural price valuation $\mathrm{d}p'/\mathrm{d}p$, as shown by Eq. (2.27):

$$\begin{aligned} &\mathrm{d}U/\mathrm{d}p = (\mathrm{d}p'/\mathrm{d}p - 1)/2tR_i \quad i = t, s, h \\ &R_t = 2, R_s = 2^{0.5}, R_h = 2/3^{0.5} \end{aligned} \tag{2.27}$$

where p' is the price of the retailer, which is located at farthest between the retailers surrounding the retailer in question. As explained in Chap. 1, when the value of $\mathrm{d}p'/\mathrm{d}p$ is 1, 0, and −1, the competition style in the retailing space is called Lösch (L),

[3]An analysis of the market area shapes under free-entry competition is carefully conducted by Ishikawa and Toda (1990).

Table 2.1a Equilibrium price and market size established in a free-entry market

F	Style	Triangle		Square		Hexagon	
		p	U	p	U	p	U
$0.01a^4$	L	$0.4557a$	$0.0963a$	$0.4583a$	$0.1091a$	$0.4589a$	$0.1171a$
	S-H	$0.1902a$	$0.1203a$	$0.1683a$	$0.1434a$	$0.1562a$	$0.1589a$
	G-O	$0.1287a$	$0.1421a$	$0.1128a$	$0.1712a$	$0.1042a$	$0.1907a$
$0.06a^4$	L	$0.3643a$	$0.2950a$	$0.3751a$	$0.3265a$	$0.3776a$	$0.3485a$
	S-H	$0.2909a$	$0.3041a$	$0.2750a$	$0.3436a$	$0.2636a$	$0.3718a$
	G-O	$0.2356a$	$0.3242a$	$0.2133a$	$0.3752a$	$0.2009a$	$0.4110a$

Hotelling-Smithies (S-H), and Greenhut-Ohta (G-O) competition, respectively. In this analysis, these three kinds of competition styles are selected as the competition styles prevailing in the plane market space.

Let us suppose that the marginal cost is zero and the two levels of the fixed cost, F, are assumed to be $0.01a^4$ and $0.06a^4$. Solving simultaneous Eq. (2.26) and (2.27) gives the competitive equilibrium price and market area size for the three different market area shapes against the two levels of fixed cost. The equilibrium values obtained by calculations are shown in Table 2.1a.

From the values of the radius of the inscribed circle of the market area, the size of the market area is derived for the three kinds of market shapes. Table 2.1b shows the equilibrium market area size for the three different market area shapes against each fixed cost level. When the market space is under Lösch competition style (L), the market shape that makes the market area size the smallest is a hexagon against each fixed cost level. When the market space is under the Greenhut-Ohta competition style (G-O), the market shape that makes the market area size the smallest is the triangle to each fixed cost level. When the market space is under the Hotelling-Smithies competition style (S-H), the market shape that makes the market area size the smallest is changed according to the fixed cost level. When the fixed cost is low, the triangular market shape makes the market area size the smallest; when the fixed cost is high, the square market shape makes the market area size the smallest.

Based on the criterion that the market shape which makes the market area size the smallest appears in a free-entry competitive equilibrium, it can be concluded

Table 2.1b Equilibrium market size established in a free-entry market

F	Style	Triangle area	Square area	Hexagon area
$0.01a^4$	L	$0.0482a^2$	$0.0476a^2$	$0.0475a^4$
	H-S	$0.075a^2$	$0.082a^2$	$0.089a^4$
	G-O	$0.011a^4$	$0.117a^2$	$0.126a^4$
$0.06a^4$	L	$0.452a^2$	$0.426a^2$	$0.421a^2$
	H-S	$0.481a^2$	$0.472a^4$	$0.479a^2$
	G-O	$0.546a^2$	$0.563a^2$	$0.585a^4$

that the three kinds of shapes have opportunity to appear in the free-entry competitive equilibrium. Which shape appears is dependent on the competition style and the fixed cost level of the retailers in the market space.

In addition, it is noteworthy that although Lösch competition style minimizes the market absolute size, the price of the retailers in Lösch competition becomes the highest irrelative market shapes. Greenhut-Ohta competition style makes the absolute market area the largest, whereas the price of the goods for retailers in Greenhut-Ohta competition becomes the lowest irrelative market shapes. Because the equilibrium profit of each retailer must be zero, the market shape problem is not so serious to each retailer. However, for every consumer, the problem of competition style among the retailers is important because the consumer surplus differs by the market shape in equilibrium.[4]

2.2.3 Shapes of Demand Curves in Retail Market Space

The retailers' prices and market areas in a free-entry competitive equilibrium vary according to the competition style among retailers. The differences in the retailers' equilibrium situations can be explained by the shapes of the demand curve in a plane market space. In this section, assuming a hexagonal market area for simplicity of the analysis, the shapes of the demand curves in plane market space are analyzed.

2.2.3.1 Demand Curved in a Greenhut-Ohta Competition Model

First, the demand curve in a Greenhut-Ohta model is examined. As shown in the above analysis, the retailers' equilibrium price and market area size in a Greenhut-Ohta model are derived by solving the simultaneous equation system of (2.25) and (2.26), assigning the value of -1 to the conjectural price valuation. In the original framework of the analysis, however, it is assumed that the delivered price at an apex of the retailer's market area is parametrically given to the retailer. Then, the competitive equilibrium price and market area are analyzed.

According to the original framework, the shape of the demand curve is examined. The quantity demanded in a retailer's market area is given by Eq. (2.28).

$$Q = 12 \int_0^{30^\circ} \int_0^{U/\cos\theta} (a - p - tu) u \, du \, d\theta \tag{2.28}$$

---

[4]See Ishikawa and Toda (1990). They shows the changes of the consumer surplus and the social surplus according the market area shape and the level of the retailers' fixed cost.

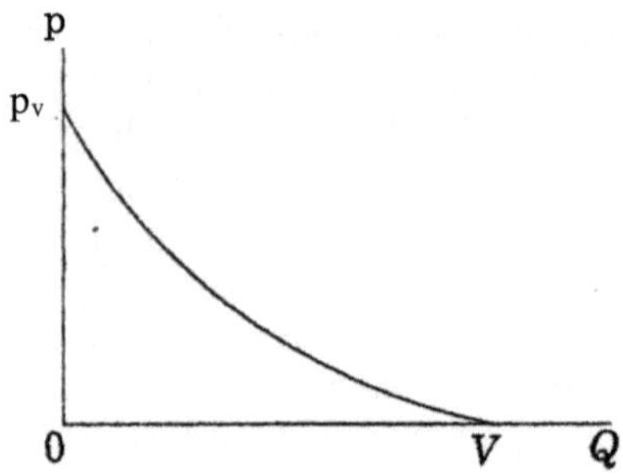

Fig. 2.4 Demand curve in Greenhut-Ohta competition model

If the delivered price at an apex is denoted by p_v, the radius of the inscribed circle of the market area U is shown by $U = 3^{0.5}/2(p_v - p)$. Thus, by integrating Eq. (2.28), the sales quantity of a retailer is given as Eq. (2.29).

$$Q = 9(p_v - p)^2\left(\left(1/2 \cdot 3^{0.5}\right)a - \left(1/2 \cdot 3^{0.5}\right)p - 0.2027(p_v - p)3^{0.5}/2\right) \quad (2.29)$$

Equation (2.29) is described by the curve p_v–V in Fig. 2.4. This curve shows the demand curve in a Greenhut-Ohta competition model.

2.2.3.2 Demand Curve in a Lösch Competition Model

Second, the demand curve in a Lösch model is examined. Here, the equilibrium price and market area size are derived by assigning the value of 1 to the conjectural price valuation. In the original framework of the analysis, it is assumed that the size of the hexagonal market area is parametrically given to a retailer. The retailers' equilibrium price and market area are derived. Thus, according to the original framework, the shape of the demand curve is examined.

Suppose that a hexagonal market area is described as points H–I–J–L–M–N in Fig. 2.5 and its radius of the inscribed circle of the market area is denoted by U. In this market area, the demand curve is shown by curve a–K'–J'–R in Fig. 2.6. This curve is explained step by step as follows.

When the retailer lowers its price at its store from the maximum reservation price a to P_k, at which the delivered price at point K in Fig. 2.5 reaches the value of a, the number of consumers increases and the quantity demanded by individual consumers is raised. The shape of the demand curve, therefore, is shown by $a-K'$ in Fig. 2.6. This shape is the same as in a case when the retailer is a monopoly.

As the retailer's price decreases toward P_j at which the delivered price at point J in Fig. 2.5 reaches just a, the demand curve is shown by $a - K'-J'$. Because that as the price reduces, the increase rate of the number of the consumers is gradually decreased by the market area border, the slope of the demand curve of $K'-J'$ is steeper than that of $a-K'$. Then, the retailer's price is reduced less than P_j; the

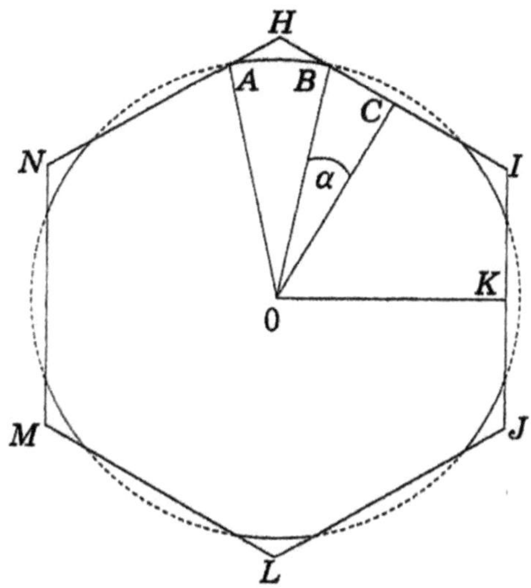

Fig. 2.5 Hexagonal marker area

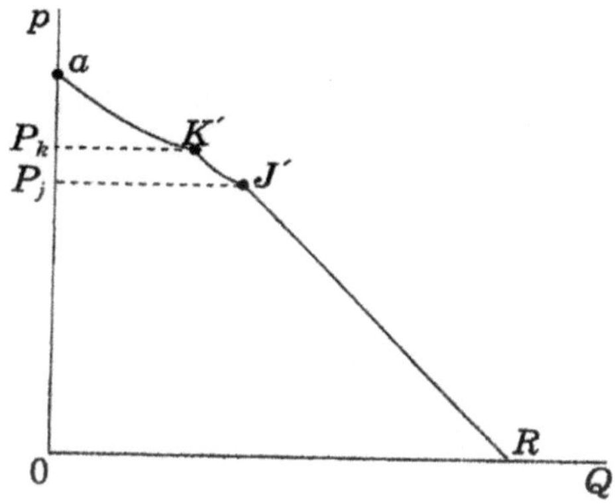

Fig. 2.6 Demand curve in a Lösch competition model

demand curve is shown by J'–R. Because the reduction of the price increases the quantity demanded by individual consumers and it does not increase the number of customers, the corresponding part of the demand curve becomes a straight line with a steeper slope. Consequently, the demand curve in a Lösch model is represented by the curve of $a-K'-J'-R$.

Let us formulate each part of the demand curve of a–$K'-J'$–R. As shown by Fig. 2.6, the demand curve of a Lösch competition model is formed by three parts. The part $a-K'$ of the demand curve is the same as that of the case when the retailer is a monopoly. Thus, the part is formulated by Eq. (2.28). In Eq. (2.28), the price p of the goods must not be higher than the price level at which the delivered price at an apex of its market is equal to the maximum demand price a.

The part $K'–J'$ of the demand curve is formulated by Eq. (2.30), which is derived by obtaining the demand quantity Q_2 in a pseudo-hexagonal market area in Fig. 2.5 as a function of price p that is in the range of $P_k > p > P_j$. The demand quantity is obtained by the summing up the quantities that are derived in the two areas of two pseudo-triangles OAB and OBC in Fig. 2.5.

$$Q_2 = 12\int_0^{\alpha}\int_0^{U/\cos\theta}(a - p - tu)u\,du\,d\theta + 6\int_0^{\pi/3-2\alpha}\int_0^{U/\cos\theta}(a - p - tu)u\,du\,d\theta \quad (2.30)$$

Here, α is the angle of BOC and $\alpha < 30^{\circ}$. Equation (2.30) is integrated as Eq. (2.31):

$$\begin{aligned} Q_2 = {} & 12U^2((\alpha/2)\tan\alpha - (p/2)\tan\alpha \\ & - (U/3)\left(\sin\alpha/\left(2\cos^2\alpha\right) + (1/2)L_N|\tan(\alpha/2 + \pi/4)|\right)) \\ & + 6U^2((\alpha/2)\tan(\pi/3 - 2\alpha) - (p/2)\tan(\pi/3 - 2\alpha) \\ & - (U/3)(\sin(\pi/3 - 2\alpha)/2\cos^2(\pi/3 - 2\alpha)) + (1/2)L_N|\tan((1/2)(\pi/3 - 2\alpha) + \pi/4)|)) \end{aligned} \quad (2.31)$$

Here, α is represented as a function of price as Eq. (2.32).

$$\alpha = \cos^{-1}(U/(a - p)) \quad (2.32)$$

Eventually, the part $K'–J$ of the demand curve is expressed as a function of price p.

Lastly, the part $J'–R$ of the demand curve is formulated as Eq. (2.33) by deriving the quantity demanded in a hexagonal market area where there is no new customer.

$$Q_3 = 12U^2\left(\left(1/2\cdot 3^{0.5}\right)a - \left(1/2\cdot 3^{0.5}\right)p - 0.2027U\right) \quad (2.33)$$

The part of $J'–R$ of the demand curve is a function of price p, which is in the range of $p < P_j$. It is expressed as a straight line.

2.2.3.3 Equilibrium Situations in Lösch and Greenhut-Ohta Competition Models

Using the two demand curves derived in the above analyses, the equilibria in Lösch and Greenhut-Ohta competition models are explained. The demand curve of Lösch model is steeper than that of a Greenhut-Ohta model. Figure 2.7 depicts these two demand curves introducing an average cost curve AC.

In Fig. 2.7, the two different equilibria are established at points E_L and E_{GO}. They show the equilibrium situations in Lösch and Greenhut-Ohta equilibria,

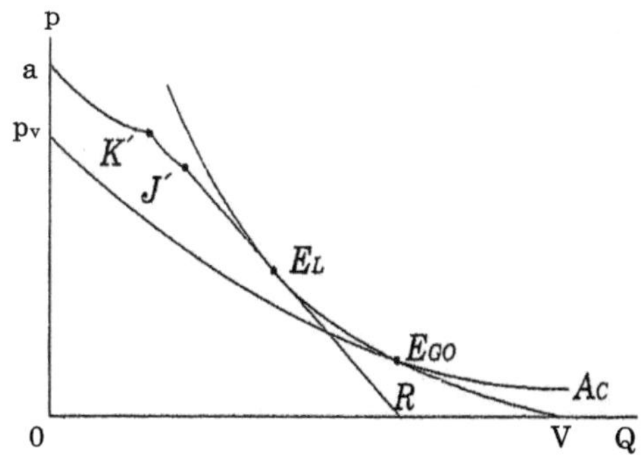

Fig. 2.7 The relationship between equilibrium values and the shape of the demand curve

respectively. As shown in Fig. 2.7, the equilibrium price of the Lösch model is always higher that of the Greenhut-Ohta model, and the quantity demanded in the Groenhut-Ohta model is larger than that of the Lösch model.

2.2.3.4 Change of Market Area Due to Decrease of Transportation Costs

This section examines the effects of a reduction of the transportation cost per mile on the competitive equilibria derived from the three kinds of the competition models.[5] In this examination, it is assumed that the retailers' market area shape is hexagon, the marginal cost is zero, the fixed cost is $0.05a^4$, and the transportation cost per mile is reduced from 1.47 to 0.2. In the same manner, the equilibrium price and inscribed radius of the market area are derived for the three kinds of the competition models. The loci of the three equilibrium situations are shown in Fig. 2.8. Table 2.2 indicates the numerical equilibrium values for the Lösch and Greenhut-Ohta competition model.

Figure 2.8 and Table 2.2 show that if the retailers are under the Greenhut-Ohta competition style, as the transportation cost per mile decreases from 1.47 to 0.2, the equilibrium price decreases and the size of the retailers' market area expands. The market area when the transportation cost per mile is 0.2 becomes larger than that of the original size. The size of the market area in the Lösch model simply squeezes as the transportation cost per mile decreases and the retail price increases. The reason for the difference in the direction of the change is the same as that shown in the analysis in a linear market space in Chap. 1.

[5]Ishikawa and Toda (1998) start to analysis the correspondence between the changes of the equilibrium situation and the competition styles.

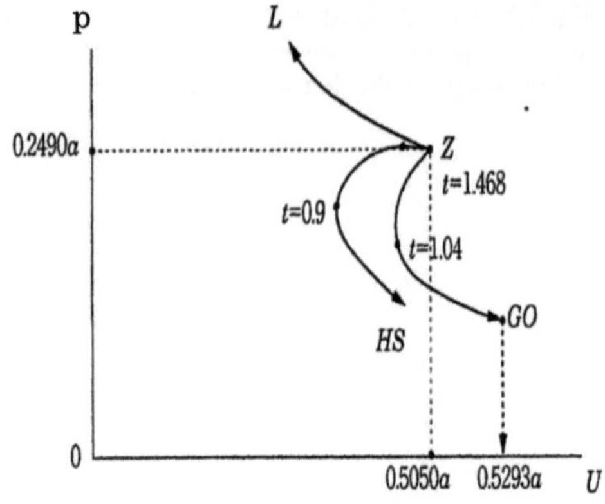

Fig. 2.8 Changes of equilibrium situations due to reducing transportation costs

Table 2.2 Changes of equilibrium values of Lösch and Greenhut-Ohta models

t	Lösch		G-O	
	U	p	U	p
1.47	0.505a	0.25a	0.505a	0.25a
1.2	0.3346a	0.3590a	0.3798a	0.2153a
1.0	0.3060a	0.3929a	0.3744a	0.1873a
0.8	0.2864a	0.4196a	0.3809a	0.1585a
0.5	0.2649a	0.4535a	0.4155a	0.1128a
0.4	0.2591a	0.4636a	0.4382a	0.0963a
0.2	0.2490a	0.4825a	0.5293a	0.060a

As the transportation cost per mile decreases, while the retailers' market area size becomes smaller than that of the original market size in a Lösch competition style, the retailers' market size becomes larger than that of the original size in a Greenhut-Ohta competition style. These facts are very important when examining the structural change of city systems that are constructed on the basis of retailers' market areas.

2.3 Effects of a Variety of Items on Retailers' Market Situations

This section discussed the variety of items in retailers' stores, analyzing the relationships between the varieties of goods at retailers' stores and market areas. Incorporating the competition styles used in the above analysis into the framework developed by Baumol and Ide (1956), this section examines the effects of the variety of items on the market boundary and the retailers' market areas in a competitive plane market space.

2.3.1 *Effects of the Variety of Items on the Boundary of Market Areas*

2.3.1.1 Assumptions and Derivation of Retailer's Profit Function

According to Baumol and Ide (1956), who systematically analyzed the relationships between the variety of items and the retailers' market areas, the following assumptions are set:

(i) Consumers evenly reside in a plane space with density *K*.
(ii) Retailers provide a number of items at their stores to consumers.
(iii) The probability that a consumer visits a retailer becomes higher as the number of the items increases. This probability, *Z*, is expressed by Eq. (2.34)[6]:

$$z(N) = (N/A_Z)^{\alpha} \tag{2.34}$$

where N is the number of the items and A_Z and α are positive parameters, respectively. The value of $Z(N)$ belongs to the range $0 \leqq Z(N) \leqq 1$.
(iv) By going to a retailer, a customer incurs some costs. The difficulty of shopping increases with the congestion of a store and with the transportation costs to the store. The congestion level, *J*, increases with the number of the items, and the transportation costs, *S*, increase with the distance to the retailer. The congestion is represented by Eq. (2.35),

$$\mathrm{J}(N) = C_n N^{\beta} \tag{2.35}$$

where C_n is the marginal cost of congestion and β is a positive parameter. The transportation cost is shown by Eq. (2.36):

$$S = tu \tag{2.36}$$

where t is the transportation cost per mile and u is the distance from a customer to a retailer's store.
(v) The willingness of a customer to visit a retailer is influenced negatively by the average price of the items, *p*. This influence, *Pa*, is expressed by Eq. (2.37)[7]:

$$Pa(p) = \phi p^{\phi} \tag{2.37}$$

where φ and φ are positive parameters.

[6]Baumol-Ide does not use a concrete function like Eq. (2.34).

[7]The average price of items is not incorporated into the analysis by Baumol and Ide (1956).

Based on these assumptions, a retailer's capacity of pulling customers, *f*, can be determined by the three factors: the number of the items *N*, the average price *p*, and the distance *u*. A retailer's capacity of pulling customers (i.e., its traction power) can be represented by Eq. (2.38):

$$f(N,p,u) = \omega(N/A_Z)^{\alpha} - \nu(C_n N^{\beta} + \mathrm{tu} + \phi p^{\varphi}) \tag{2.38}$$

where ω and v are positive parameters.

(vi) The quantity demanded in a retailer's market area is proportional to the traction power of attracting customers to the retailer's store. When a retailer's market area is a circle, the quantity demanded, Q, in its market area is expressed by Eq. (2.39):

$$Q = 2\pi \int_0^U ((N/A_Z)^{\alpha} - \nu(\mathrm{tu} + C_n N^{\beta} + \varphi p^{\phi}))u du \tag{2.39}$$

where U is the radius of the circular market area. Because the average price of the items is represented by p, the retailer's revenue, Rv, is derived by Eq. (2.40):

$$Rv = pQ. \tag{2.40}$$

(vii) Inventory costs of the retailer are shown by Eq. (2.41):

$$\mathrm{IC} = (E/I)r + (I/2 + R)T, \tag{2.41}$$

where E is the expected sales volume of all commodities per period, r is the handling costs of reordering, I is the quantity ordered for inventory each time stocks are replaced, T is the warehousing cost per item per period, and R is the stock level at which inventory is replaced (i.e., the stocks on hand fall to R and the retailer replaces inventory). From Eq. (2.41), the optimal inventory (*ICI*) per item is derived by Eq. (2.42):

$$\mathrm{ICI} = (2rTQ/N)^{0.5} + \mathrm{RT}. \tag{2.42}$$

(viii) The fixed costs of the warehouse and the retail facility are shown by F. The dealing costs of goods are proportional to the number of the items, and the costs are expressed as $eN^{0.5}$, where e is the parameter. The total costs of a retailer are given by Eq. (2.43):

$$\mathrm{TC} = N(2rTQ/N)^{0.5} + \mathrm{NRT} + \mathrm{eN}^{0.5} + F. \tag{2.43}$$

Finally, the retailer's profit, Y, is given by Eq. (2.44):

$$\begin{aligned} Y = p(2\pi \mathrm{KU}^2(0.5(\omega(N/A_Z)^\alpha - \nu C_n N^\beta - \nu\phi p^\varnothing) - \mathrm{vtU}/3)) \\ - N^{0.5}((2\mathrm{rT}(2\pi K\, U^2(0.5(\omega(N/Az)^\alpha - \nu C_n\, N^\beta - \nu\varphi p^\varnothing) \\ - \mathrm{vtU}/3)))^{0.5} + e) - \mathrm{NRT} - F \end{aligned} \tag{2.44}$$

2.3.1.2 Effect of a Variety of Items on the Market Area Boundary

Before conducting the analysis of the market area boundary, let us examine the retailer's capacity of pulling customers when the variety of the items is considered.

We assigned the following numerical values to the parameters in Eq. (2.38): $A_Z = 20$, $\omega = 45$, $v = 5.6667$, $t = 0.2$, $Cn = 1.2$, $\alpha = 0.26$, $\beta = 0.5$, $\varphi = 0.2$, and $\varnothing = 1.05$. The retailer's capacity of pulling customers is then given by Eq. (2.45):

$$f(N,p,u) = 45(N/20)^{0.26} - 5.6667\left(0.2u + 1.2N^{0.5} + 0.2p^{1.05}\right) \tag{2.45}$$

When one retailer is located in a plane space, the retailer's market area is established by points at which the retailer's traction power of customers is zero; that is, Eq. (2.45) is zero at these points. For example, assume that the retailer is located at the origin of the coordinates of x and y, the number of the items N is 0.5, and the average price p is 4.0. The points at which the retailer's power to pull customers is zero are derived by solving Eq. (2.46) with respect to x and y.

$$f(x,y) = 45(0.5/20)^{0.26} - 5.6667\left(0.2(x^2+y^2)^{0.5} + 1.2\cdot 0.5^{0.5} + 0.2\cdot 4^{1.05}\right) = 0 \tag{2.46}$$

In this case, the retailer's market area is indicated by a circle, which is depicted by the larger circle in Fig. 2.9. The radius U of the circle is 6.69. If the number of the items N decreases to 0.1, the circular market area shrinks to the small circle with the radius of 3.83, which is shown by the smaller circle in Fig. 2.9. Keeping the average price at the same level, the reduction in the number of the items shrinks the retailer's market area by 95.53. This shrunken area reveals the effect of the variety of the items on the size of the retailer's market area.

Now, let us suppose that two rival retailers A and B are in a plane market space. Retailer A and B are located at points (−2, 0) and (2, 0), respectively. It is also assumed that the retailers' varieties of the items are denoted by N_A and N_B; their transportation costs per mile and the average prices are represented by t_A, t_B and p_A, p_B, respectively.

The market area boundary of the two retailers is formed by points where the two retailers' powers to attract customers are the same. Equation (2.47) must be satisfied at the market area boundary:

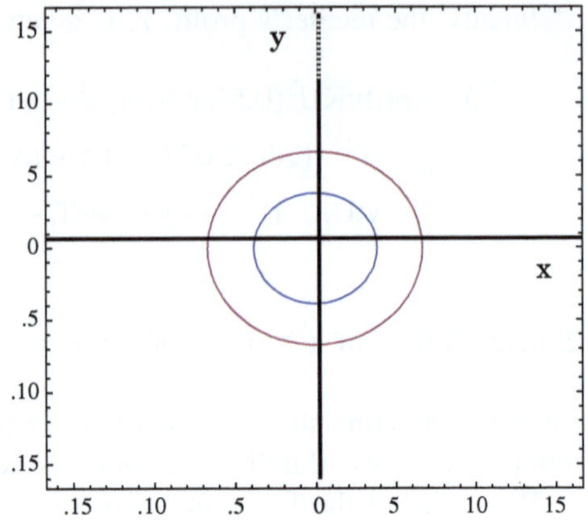

Fig. 2.9 Formation of a retailer's market area

$$45(N_A/20)^{0.26} - 5.6667\left(t_A\left((x+2)^2+y^2\right)^{0.5} + 1.2N_A^{0.5} + 0.2p_A^{1.05}\right)$$
$$= 45(N_B/20)^{0.26} - 5.6667\left(t_B\left((x-2)^2+y^2\right)^{0.5} + 1.2N_B^{0.5} + 0.2p_B^{1.05}\right) \tag{2.47}$$

Supposing that $N_A = N_B = 0.98$, $t_A = t_B = 0.2$, $p_A = p_B = 1.1$, the market area boundary is obtained by Eq. (2.47). In this case, the market area boundary is a straight line, as shown by the line in Fig. 2.10. Then, when the number of the items stocked at the store of retailer A increases from 0.98 to 1.27, keeping the average prices of both retailers at the same level, the boundary becomes a hyperbola, which is represented in Fig. 2.10. Retailer A expands its market area toward retailer B.

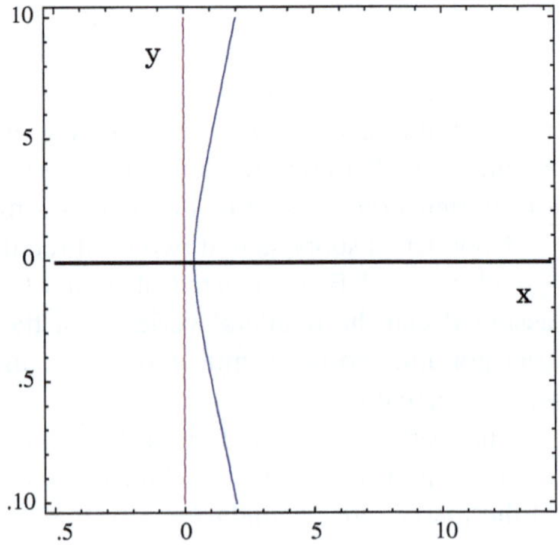

Fig. 2.10 Market area boundaries indicated by a straight line and a hyperbola

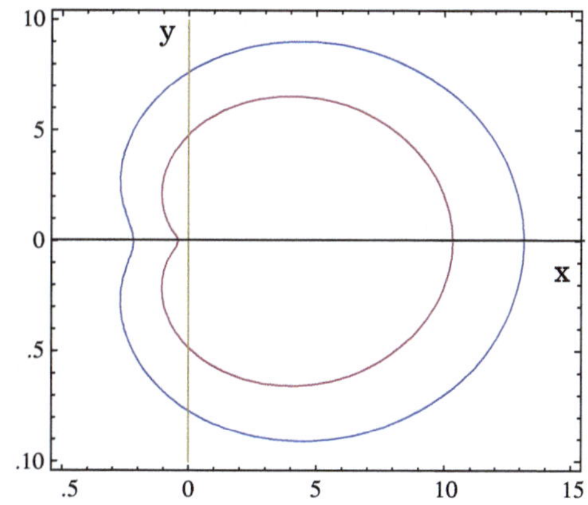

Fig. 2.11 Market area boundary indicated by ellipses

On this boundary, the delivered average price level of retailer A is higher than that of retailer B. Because retailer A provides more variety of items than its rival retailer B, retailer A occupies a larger market area than retailer B.

Then, assume that retailers A and B are located at (−0.5, 0) and (0.5, 0), respectively, and that the number of items are the same between the retailers, $N_A = N_B = 0.98$. The average price and transportation cost per mile are different between the retailers: $p_A = 2$, $p_B = 1.1$, and $t_A = 0.2$, $t_B = 0.24$. In this case, the market boundary is depicted by the small closed ellipse in Fig. 2.11. The area enclosed by the small ellipse is the market area of retailer B. When the number of the items of retailer B increases to $N_B = 1.37$, the market area boundary expands to the large ellipse in Fig. 2.11. The increase of the variety of the items expands the market area of retailer *B*. It can be said that incorporating the variety of the items stocked at the retailers' stores into consideration gives the flexibility of the market area analyses and provides the ability to explain the locations and the market areas of the retailers in the real world.

2.3.2 *Effect of the Variety of Items on Retailers' Market Area Size*

2.3.2.1 Influence of Competition Styles on the Equilibrium for the Variety of Items

Assuming that free-entry competition among the retailers prevails in a plane market space, this section derives the number of the items, the average price of the items, and the market area size in a spatial free-entry equilibrium.

There are three conditions for a free-entry equilibrium to be established in a spatial free-entry market space when the variety of the items in the retailers' stores is included in the preceding framework of the analysis. Every retailer determines the number of the items and the average price to maximize its profit. A new retailer comes into the market space until every retailer's profit is just zero. These conditions are shown by Eqs. (2.48a, b, c):

$$\partial Y/\mathrm{d}N = \partial Y/\partial N + \partial Y/\partial U \cdot \partial U/\partial N = 0 \tag{2.48a}$$

$$\partial Y/\mathrm{d}p = \partial Y/\partial p + \partial Y/\partial U \cdot \partial U/\partial p = 0 \tag{2.48b}$$

$$Y = 0 \tag{2.48c}$$

In Eq. (2.48a), $\partial U/\partial N$ represents the variation of the radius of the market area when a retailer changes the number of the items by one unit; $\partial U/\partial N$ and $\partial U/\partial N$ are given by Eqs. (2.49a), (b), respectively:

$$\partial U/\partial N = \left(\left((\omega/\nu)(\alpha/A^{\alpha})\mathrm{N}^{\alpha-1} - \beta C_n \mathrm{N}^{\beta-1}\right)/2t\right)(1 - \mathrm{d}N'/\mathrm{d}N) \tag{2.49a}$$

$$\partial U/\partial p = ((1/2t)\varphi\phi p^{\phi-1)})(1 - \mathrm{dp}'/\mathrm{dp}) \tag{2.49b}$$

where N' in Eq. (2.49a) is the rival retailer's number of the items and dN'/dN is the conjectural variation of the variety.

When the value of dN'/dN equals 1, the Lösch competition style is indicated in terms of the items. In this case, when a retailer increases an item at the store, the retailer conjectures that the rival also increases one item at its store. Assuming that the values of dN'/dN and dp'/dp are 1 and solving the simultaneous Eqs. (2.48a, b, c) with respect to N, p, and U, the number of the items, the average price, and the market area size in the Lösch equilibrium are obtained. When the values of dN'/dN and dp'/dp are assumed to be 0, it indicates Hotelling-Smithies competition style; in the same way, the values can be obtained for the Hotelling-Smithies equilibrium.

For the values of the Lösch and Hotelling-Smithies equilibria, the following numerical values were assigned to parameters; $A_Z = 20$, $F = 20$, $K = 1.75$, $R = 5$, $T = 2$, $e = 0.15$, $r = 1.6$, $\alpha = 0.26$, $\omega = 45$, $v = 5.6667$, $t = 1.2$, $\varphi = 0.2$, $\varnothing = 1.05$, $\beta = 0.5$, and $C_n = 1.2$. First, the retailer's profit function Y is shown by Eq. (2.50).

$$\begin{aligned} Y = {} & p\left(2 \cdot 3.14 \cdot 1.75U^2\left(0.5\left(45(N/20)^{0.26} - (5.6667 \cdot 1.2)N^{0.5} - (5.6667 \cdot 2p^{1.05})\right)\right.\right. \\ & \left.\left. -(5.6667 \cdot 1.2/3)U\right)\right) - 20 - N^{0.5}\left(\left(2 \cdot 3.14 \cdot 1.75U^2\left(0.5\left(45(N/20)^{0.26} - 6.8N^{0.5}\right.\right.\right.\right. \\ & \left.\left.\left.\left. -(5.6667 \cdot 0.2p^{1.05})\right)\right) - (5.6667 \cdot 1.2/3)U\right)\right)^{0.5} + 0.15\right) - N \cdot 5 \cdot 2 \end{aligned} \tag{2.50}$$

Then, $\partial Y/\partial N$ and $\partial Y/\partial p$ are given by Eqs. (2.51a), (b):

$$\begin{aligned}\partial Y/\partial N = & -10+5.49778(5.3693/N^{0.74}-3.40002/N^{0.5})\mathrm{pU}^2 \\ & -(2.09719(5.3693/N^{0.74}-3.4/N^{0.5})N^{0.5}U^2)/((0.5(20.6512N^{0.26} \\ & -6.8N^{0.5}-1.13334p^{1.05})-2.26668U)U^2)^{0.5}-(0.5(0.15+8.38878 \\ & ((0.5(20.6512N^{0.26}-6.8N^{0.5}-1.13334p^{1.05})-2.26668U)U^2)^{0.5}))/N^{0.5}\end{aligned} \tag{2.51a}$$

$$\begin{aligned}Y/\partial p = & -6.5424p^{1.05}U^2+10.9956(0.5(20.6512N^{0.26} \\ & -6.80004N^{0.5}-1.13334p^{1.05})-2.26668U)U^2 \\ & +(2.49568N^{0.5}p^{0.05}U^2)/((0.5(20.6512N^{0.26}-6.8N^{0.5} \\ & -1.13334p^{1.05})-2.26668U)U^2)^{0.5}\end{aligned} \tag{2.51b}$$

Lastly, the term $\partial Y/\partial U$ in Eqs. (2.48a), (b) is derived as Eq. (2.52):

$$\begin{aligned}\partial Y/\partial U = & 21.9911p(0.5(20.6512N^{0.26}-6.80004N^{0.5}-1.13334p^{1.05}) \\ & -2.26668U)U-24.9234pU^2-(4.19439N^{0.5}(2(0.5(20.6512N^{0.26} \\ & -6.8N^{0.5}-1.13334p^{1.05})-2.26668U)U-2.26668U^2))/((0.5(20.65128N^{0.26}-6.8N^{0.5} \\ & -1.13334p^{1.05})-2.26668U))(U^2)^{0.5}\end{aligned} \tag{2.52}$$

Now, using the above four equations, Eqs. (2.48a, b, c) can be rewritten to be calculable. Solving the simultaneous equations system (2.48a, b, c) with respect to N, p, and U gives the equilibrium number of the items, the average price, and the market area size.[8] The equilibrium values are shown in Table 2.3.

When the transportation costs per mile decreases from 1.2 to 0.2, the equilibrium values of the retailer are changed. In this case, the equilibrium values are shown in Table 2.4.

By comparing the figures shown in Tables 2.3 and 2.4, it is found that the number of the items in the Hotelling-Smithies equilibrium is higher than that of Lösch equilibrium, the average price in Hotelling-Smithies is lower than Lösch, and the market area size in Hotelling-Smithies is larger than Lösch. In addition, the changes of the equilibrium values due to the decrease of the transportation cost per mile are different according to the competition style between the retailers. When Lösch competition prevails among the retailers, because the transportation costs are lower, the number of the items decreases and the market area size shrinks; in

[8]In this analysis, the Greenhut-Ota competition style is not selected because the main purpose of this subsection is to show that the difference of the competition styles influences the retailers' market situations.

Table 2.3 The equilibrium number of items, average price, and market area size

Competition style	Item N	Average price p	Market area size U
Lösch	1.081	4.894	0.506
H-S	2.822	7.011	0.659

H-S: Hotelling-Smithies competition style

Table 2.4 The equilibrium values when the transportation costs is low

Competition style	Item N	Average price p	Market area size U
Lösch	0.881	5.491	0.422
H-S	5.188	10.941	1.035

H-S: Hotelling-Smithies competition style

Hotelling-Smithies competition, the number of the items increases and the market area size expands.

2.3.2.2 Changes of the Number of Items and Market Size by Decreasing Transportation Costs

Now, by observing the retail types in the real world, the retailer's types could be roughly classified into three categories: convenience store, supermarket store, and department store. It is possible to assign conjectural variations of the item and of the price to the competition style prevailing in each category. The distances between convenience stores are short and they deal with small goods with low prices. Thus, the conjectural variation of item and price would be assumed as $dp'/dp = 1$ and $dN'/dN = 1$—that is, a Lösch competition style. The distances between supermarkets are relatively long and they deal with daily goods with low and medium prices. Thus, it is possible to assume that dp'/dp is 1, and the conjectural variation of the item is $dN'/dN = 0.75$. A supermarket store assumes that when it changes the number of items by one unit, the rival store changes the number of items by 0.75 because the rival cannot immediately change the number of the items to the same level. It is assumed in the case of department stores that the conjectural variations are $dp'/dp = -0.5$ and $dN/dN = -0.25$. Customers visit a department store to purchase goods with high prices and they attach great importance to their taste. The department store attempts to provide many varieties of goods and plans to sell the goods by differentiating from their rivals. Thus, the department store assumes that against the change of the number of the items and the average price of its store, the rival takes the opposite response. Hence, in this analysis, it is assumed that the department store sets the conjectural variations of the items and price as $dp'/dp = -0.5$ and $dN'/dN = -0.25$ in order to maximize its profits.[9]

[9]Schöler (1993) shows the cases that the conjectural variation of price takes a negative value.

Then, because the fixed costs, the number of the variety, and some parameters' values seems to be different between the three retailing types, this section assumes the following values:

- For convenience stores, $F = 5$, $A_Z = 20$, $R = 5$, $r = 1.5$, and $\omega = 40$
- For supermarkets, $F = 27$, $A_Z = 20$, $R = 20$, $r = 1.5$, and $\omega = 42$
- For department stores, $F = 30$, $A_Z = 16$, $R = 10$, $r = 1.7$, and $\omega = 46$.

Other values of parameters are assumed to be the same for simplicity of the analysis. By lowering the transportation cost per mile from 0.6 to 0.2, the equilibrium market values are derived for the three retail types at each level of the transportation costs. The results are shown in Tables 2.5a, b, c, respectively.

The comparison of the figures shown in these three tables gives the following interesting facts: the market area of the convenience stores becomes smaller and the number of the variety stocked in the stores decreases as the transportation cost per mile lowers. The market area of the supermarket stores becomes smaller until transportation costs per mile lower to 0.4 and it begins to expand by a reduction in

Table 2.5a Changes of the equilibrium values of a convenience store

t	N	P	U
0.6	0.140	1.883	0.391
0.5	0.136	1.914	0.382
0.4	0.132	1.945	0.374
0.3	0.129	1.974	0.367
0.2	0.126	2.002	0.360

Table 2.5b Changes of the equilibrium values of a supermarket

t	N	p	U
0.6	0.689	4.211	0.738
0.5	0.822	4.55	0.731
0.4	0.847	4.585	0.712
0.3	1.056	4.831	0.720
0.2	1.389	5.097	0.745

Table 2.5c Changes of the equilibrium values of a department store

t	N	p	U
0.6	5.085	10.763	0.979
0.5	5.471	11.229	1.036
0.4	5.912	11.724	1.113
0.3	6.424	12.262	1.224
0.2	7.042	12.864	1.402

the transportation costs; the number of the items stocked in the stores increases by decreasing transportation costs. The number of the items stocked in department stores increases and the market areas expand as the transportation cost per mile lowers.

It is interesting to know that changes of the number of the items and the market area size due to the reduction of the transportation cost are greatly different between the retail store types.

2.3.3 *The Difference in Traction Powers at a Store and the Market Boundary*

This section examines the retailer's capacity to pull customers (i.e., its traction power) at its store and at the market area boundary. Figure 2.12 illustrates the traction powers at the store's location for the three kinds of the retailers against the six different transport cost levels from 0.6 to 0.2. The supermarket store's traction power, which is denoted by the square mark, is the highest between the three kinds of stores. Its traction power changes in a U-shape as the transport cost decreases. The department store's traction power, which is denoted by the triangle mark, is the lowest between them. The convenience store's power, which is denoted by the diamond mark, is between the supermarket and the department store.

Figure 2.13 illustrates the traction powers at the market area boundary for the three kinds of retailers against the six transport cost levels. The supermarket store's traction power at the market area is the highest between the three kinds of stores. Its traction power increases as the transport cost decreases. The department store's traction power is the lowest between them. The traction powers of both the supermarket store and the convenience store increase as the transport cost decreases. The department store's power decreases as the transport cost is reduced.

Figure 2.14 shows the difference between the traction powers at the store and at the market area boundary for the three kinds of retailers against the six transport

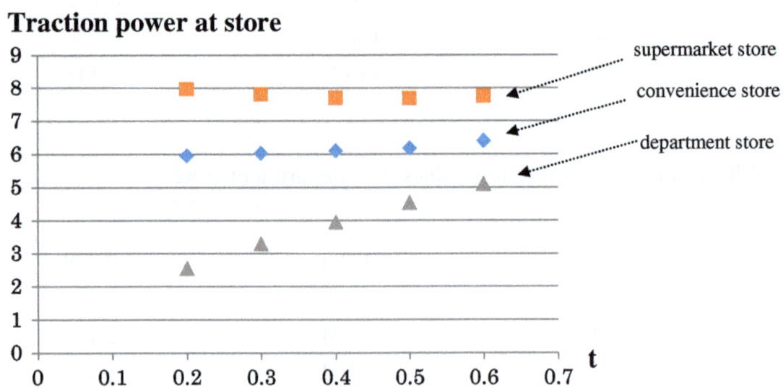

Fig. 2.12 Retailers' capacity to pull customers at the store

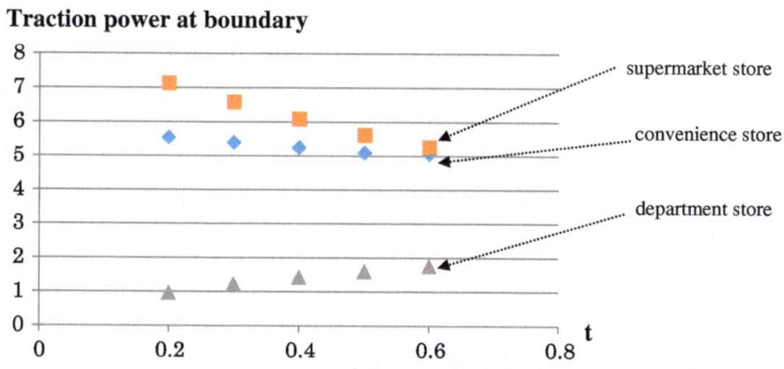

Fig. 2.13 Retailers' capacity to pull customers at the boundary

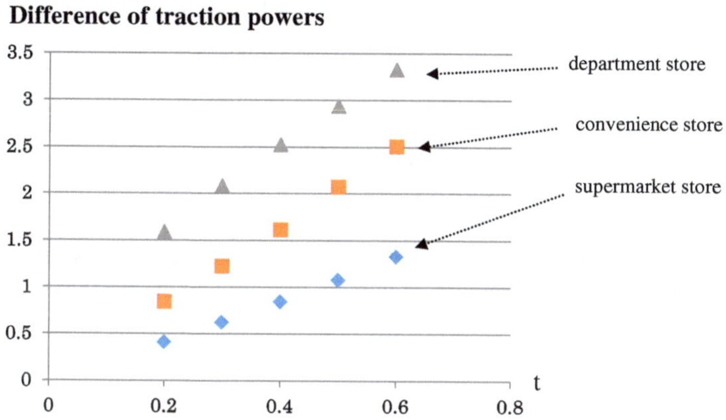

Fig. 2.14 Difference of the traction powers at the store and the boundary

cost levels from 0.6 to 0.2. The difference of the traction powers of every kind of retailer becomes small as the transport cost reduces. Although the directions of the change of the number of the items, the market size, and the average price of the items are different between the three kinds of the stores, there is a common trend between them: the difference of the traction powers at the stores' location and at the market area boundary becomes smaller as the transportation cost decreases.

2.4 Effects of Freight Rate on Items and Market of a Shopping Center

Since Dixit-Stiglitz's work (1977) on production and utility functions, a variety of items has been incorporated into the analysis of the retail industry. By using the utility function developed by Dixit-Stiglitz, many studies have provided useful insights about the economic effects of the variety of items on the locations of the retailers inducing the operations of shopping centers in a plane market space. Henkel-Stahl-Walz (2000) incorporated the diversification of items into the utility function of consumers and examined the influence of the number of the items on the market area of the shopping center. This section incorporates the concept of the interaction between the shopping centers and analyzes, utilizing the framework that Henkel-Stahl-Walz built, the relationship between the variety of the items and the market areas of shopping centers.

2.4.1 Assumptions and Framework

This section sets the following assumptions. Consumers are equally distributed over a plane space with a density of 1. Each consumer has a utility function G, which is shown by Eq. (2.53):

$$G = \left[\int_0^n q(i,u)^{\sigma - 1/\sigma} \mathrm{d}i \right]^{\sigma/\sigma - 1} \tag{2.53}$$

where $q\ (i,\ u)$ is the quantity demanded for goods i, which depends on the distance u from a consumer to the retailer at which the consumer purchases the goods' n denotes the number of the items of the retailer; σ is a parameter; and $\sigma > 1$. The constraint of the budget is shown by Eq. (2.54):

$$y = \int_0^n p(i) q(i,u) \mathrm{d}i + tu \tag{2.54}$$

where y is the consumer's income, $p(i)$ is the price of goods i, and t denotes the transportation cost per mile. Each consumer purchases goods while aiming at maximization of their utility under the income restraint shown by Eq. (2.54). The quantity demanded for goods i is given by Eq. (2.55):

$$\mathrm{q(i)} = \frac{p_i^{-\sigma}}{\int_0^n p(i)^{1-\sigma} \mathrm{d}i} (y - tu) \tag{2.55}$$

Because a kind of good is supplied by a retailer, the number of kinds of goods, n, implies the number of retailers. Each retailer is located at a shopping center, which occupies the central sales place of a city. A retailer sets a price to maximize its profit at the shopping center. There is not a manager who dictates the shopping center. Hence, retailers can enter into the shopping center until a retailer's profit becomes just zero. The market area of the shopping center is expanded to points where consumers give up visiting the shopping center. The shape of the market area is given by a circle with the radius, *U*.

The retailer that sells the goods, *i*, at the shopping center obtains the profit *Y*(*i*), which is shown by Eq. (2.56):

$$Y(i) = 2\pi \int_0^U (p(i) - c)q(i, u)\mathrm{d}u - F \tag{2.56}$$

where *c* and *F* are the marginal and fixed costs, respectively.

Because each retailer sets the price to maximize its profit, the price of goods, *i*, is given by Eq. (2.57):

$$p = c\sigma/(\sigma - 1) \tag{2.57}$$

where *p* is the *representative* price of all kinds of goods at the shopping center. Because the quantity demanded by a consumer is given by Eq. (2.55), the retailer's profit is rewritten by Eq. (2.57a):

$$Y(i) = (2\pi/n\sigma) \int_0^U (y - tu)u\mathrm{d}u - F \tag{2.57a}$$

The retailer's profit is eventually shown by a function of the radius of the market area, as shown by Eq. (2.57b):

$$Y(i) = (2\pi/n\sigma)U^2(y - tU/2) - F \tag{2.57b}$$

Because a retailer can enter into the shopping center until its profit become to zero, the equilibrium number of the retailers at the shopping center, n^*, is derived by Eq. (2.57b) as a function of the radius of the market area as Eq. (2.58):

$$n^* = 2\pi U^2(y - tU/2)/\sigma F \tag{2.58}$$

The utility of the consumer who comes to the shopping center must not be negative. Thus, the inverse utility of the consumer who comes to the shopping center is derived as Eq. (2.59):

$$V = \left(\frac{\sigma - 1}{c\sigma}\right)(2\pi u^2(y - tu/2)/\sigma F)^{\frac{1}{\sigma-1}}(y - tu) \tag{2.59}$$

The market area cannot be expanded beyond the site at which the retailer's profit becomes zero. In addition, it is clarified that the market area is not expanded to cross the point where the utility of a consumer becomes just zero.

2.4.2 The Number of Retailers and Market Area of a Shopping Center

Let us derive the number of the retailers, the market area size, and the level of utility of a consumer by numerical calculation. The following numerical values were assigned to the parameters: the transport cost per mile, $t = 1.2$; parameter, $\sigma = 5$; fixed cost, $F = 25$, and consumer's income, $y = 50$. Under this situation, from Eq. (2.58), the relationship between the number of the retailers and the market area size is illustrated in Fig. 2.15. When the radius of the market area of the shopping center is 55.55, the number of the retailers is maximized at $n = 2585.7$. The utility of a consumer who resides at an end-point of the market area is shown in Fig. 2.16.

As shown in Fig. 2.16, when the radius of the shopping center's market area is 41.67, the utility of the consumers who reside at the boundary of the market area becomes just zero. Thus, the radius of the market area is determined by that size. The number of retailers is 2181.7 when the size of the market area of the shopping center is $U = 41.67$. This market area size is less than that of the market area that makes the retailer's profit just zero, $U = 55.55$. When the radius of the market area is determined at 41.67, the level of utility of each consumer in the market area is shown by Fig. 2.17 as a function of the distance from the shopping center to each consumer. As shown by Fig. 2.17, the consumer residing next to the shopping center enjoys the highest utility of 195.3, while the utility of the consumer who lives at the boundary of the market area becomes zero.

Fig. 2.15 The change of the number of retailers due to the expansion of the market area

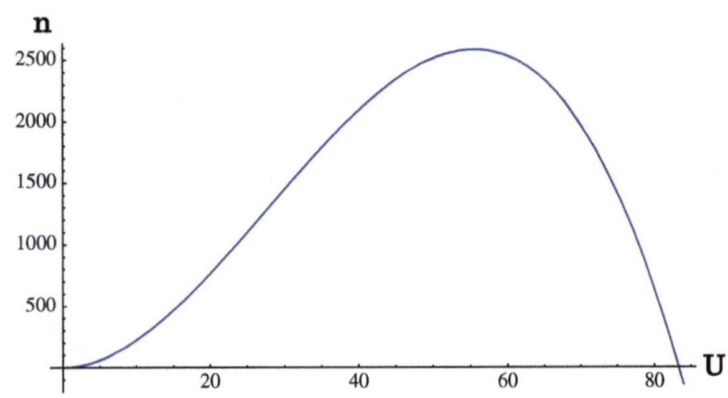

Fig. 2.16 The utility level of the consumer at the boundary of the market area

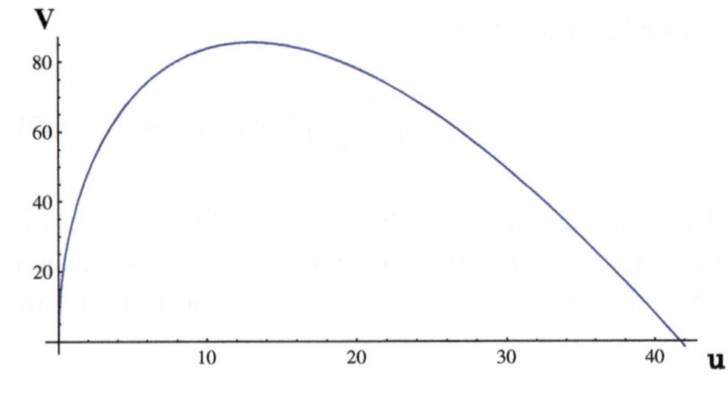

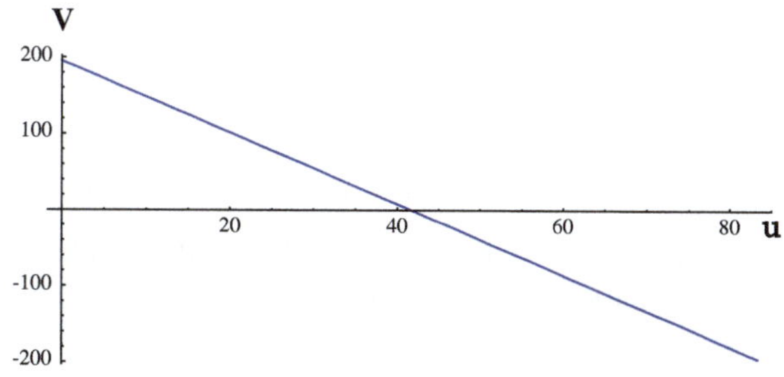

Fig. 2.17 The relationship between a consumer's utility and distance from the shopping center

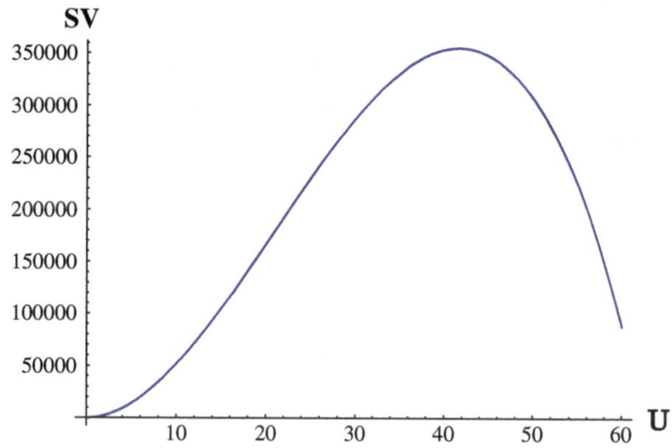

Fig. 2.18 The relationship between total utility and the market area size

Finally, let us examine the variation of the total utility of all consumers, *SV*, as the market area of the shopping center expands. The variation is illustrated in Fig. 2.18. As illustrated by Fig. 2.18, the total utility of all consumers is maximized, SV = 355,006, at the market size of $U = 41.67$. Thus, the boundary of the market area becomes settled at point where the utility of the consumers becomes just zero; such a market area size maximizes the total utility of all consumers in the market area.

2.4.3 *Change of the Number of Retailers at Centers Due to Decreasing Freight Rates*

2.4.3.1 Change of the Framework of the Analysis

In the following analysis, additional assumptions are set as follows:

1. Many shopping centers are in a plane market space. Their market area shape is a circle.
2. Each shopping center is dictated by a manager who can adjust the number of retailers located at the center to maximize every retailer's profit.

3. The competition between the shopping centers arises; then, the market areas of the shopping centers are forced to be reduced to the size that makes the profit of each retailer becomes just zero.
4. Every shopping center moves instantly without any costs. The location of every center adjusts to establish an equilibrium situation.

Under these assumptions, the number of the retailers at the shopping center and the center's market area size and consumer's utility are analyzed.

2.4.3.2 Analysis of a Shopping Center in a Monopolistic Competition

Because the manager of a shopping center can adjust the number of the retailers to maximize every retailer's profit, the manger determines the number of the retailers to satisfy Eq. (2.60):

$$\partial Y_i/\partial n_A = \left(2\pi U/\left(\sigma n_A^2\right)\right)\left(-yU + tU^2/2 + n_A(2y - 3tU/2)\mathrm{d}U/\mathrm{d}n_A\right) = 0 \tag{2.60}$$

Here, $\mathrm{d}U/\mathrm{d}n_A$ is determined by Eq. (2.61):

$$\mathrm{d}U/\mathrm{d}n_A = (1/(\sigma - 1))n_A^{(2-\sigma)/(\sigma-1)}(\mathrm{y} - \mathrm{tU_A})/\left(2\mathrm{tn}_A^{1/(\sigma-1)}\right) \times (1 - \mathrm{d}n_B/\mathrm{d}n_A) \tag{2.61}$$

where n_A is the number of the retailers at shopping center A and n_B is the number of the retailers at the rival shopping center B, which exists nearest to shopping center A.

dn_B/dn_A is the value forecasted by the manager of shopping center A. The conjectural variation of number (CVN) of the rival shopping center B is when shopping center A changes the number of the retailers at the center A. As mentioned in the preceding analysis, the value of CVN is usually assumed to be $-1 \leqq \text{CVN} \leqq 1$. The typically assumed values are 1, 0, and −1. When the value of dn_B/dn_A equals 1, the Lösch competition style is indicated. The values 0 and −1 give the Hotelling-Smithies and the Greenhut-Ohta competition styles, respectively. These three typical competition styles are assumed in this analysis.

Because a monopolistic competition arises between the shopping centers, the profit of every retailer at each shopping center must be zero. Thus, the market area size of each shopping center is forced to have a market area size that makes the retailer's profit zero. This equilibrium condition is given by Eq. (2.62):

$$Y(i) = (2\pi/n_A\sigma)U^2(y - tU/2) - F = 0 \tag{2.62}$$

The number of retailers and the market area size of the shopping center under a monopolistic competition equilibrium is derived by solving Eqs. (2.60) and (2.62) with respect to n_A and U. Assigning the same values used in the above analysis to the parameters and lowering the freight rates from 1.2 to 0.8 by the interval 0.2, the equilibrium number of the retailers and the radius of the market area are obtained. The equilibrium values for the three competition styles are shown in Table 2.6. The following interesting facts are obtained from Table 2.6. Due to a decline of the transportation cost per mile, the number of the retailers increases and the market area of the shopping center expands in Hotelling-Smithies and Greenhut-Ohta competition styles. While in Lösch competition style, the number of retailers decreases and the market area shrinks.

When the transportation cost per mile is high and the competition style between the shopping centers is the Lösch type, the number of the retailers is the highest and the market area is the largest. On the other hand, when the competition style is the Hotelling-Smithies type, the number of the retailers is lowest and the market area is the smallest. When the transportation cost per mile is low, in the Greenhut-Ohta competition style, the number of the retailers is the highest and the market area becomes the largest. It is interesting that as the transportation cost per mile declines, whether the number of the retailers at the shopping center increases or decreases is dependent on the competition style between the shopping centers. Similarly, the market area size is also influenced by the competition style.

Then, the total utility level of all the consumers, SV, and the utility level per person, *vp*, in a market area of a shopping center can be derived against each freight rate. Table 2.7 shows the interesting results: As the transportation cost per mile falls, the total utility of all consumers increases in the Hotelling-Smithies and Greenhut-Ohta competition styles, while it decreases in the case of Lösch style. The utility level per person goes up for the three competition styles. When the transportation cost per mile is high, the competition style that maximizes the utility level per person is the Lösch style. Conversely, when the transportation cost per mile is low, the utility is maximized in the Greenhut-Ohta competition style.

Table 2.6 Change of the number of retailers and market due to decreasing freight rates

t	Lösch		Hotelling-Smithies		Greenhut-Ohta	
	n	U	n	U	n	U
1.2	402.2	13.9	114.6	8.0	358.8	13.0
1.0	345.8	12.6	208.2	9.6	516.6	15.6
0.8	311.8	11.8	325.4	12.0	807.2	19.5

Table 2.7 Change of utility of consumers due to decreasing transportation costs per mile

t	Lösch		Hotelling-Smithies		Greenhut-Ohta	
	SV	vp	SV	vp	SV	vp
1.2	60,243	99.5	16,314	81.5	52,287	98.5
1.0	50,981	102.5	27,243	94.7	82,571	107.9
0.8	45,692	105.0	47,647	105.9	144,086	120.6

2.4.3.3 The Importance of an Expanding Market Area in an Equilibrium

In the real world, the locations of shopping centers cannot move easily. If the transportation cost per mile becomes lower, the equilibrium market area size of the shopping centers becomes larger. This fact has an important economic meaning: As innovation in transportation progresses, the freight rate gradually falls. When the competition style between the shopping centers is the Hotelling-Smithies type, the number of the retailers at the shopping centers increases and the necessitated spatial size of their market areas expands. This implies that some shopping centers are eventually forced to leave from the market space. Therefore, the structure of the retail systems established in the early stages of economic development is altered as economic development progresses to a certain stage: The decreasing transportation cost collapses the spatial organization of the existing competitive equilibrium of the retailers and the shopping centers. This alters the existing city systems in a market space and provides the surviving retailers with positive profits.

Chapter 3
Market Analysis Using the Contact Price Curve

There are infinite competitive equilibria in a spatial free-entry competition market in the retail industry. Among them, the retailers' market area size and price of goods in Lösch and Greenhut-Ohta competitive equilibria have conspicuous characteristics. Surprisingly, these two interesting equilibria with clear features can be easily derived using the contact price curve (CPC). This chapter shows that the two equilibria correspond to two special points of the CPC.

3.1 Derivation of Spatial Free-Entry Equilibria Using an Existing Method

3.1.1 Derivation of Lösch Equilibrium in Spatial Free-Entry Market Space

In this chapter, it is assumed that a kind of good is sold by many retailers to a plane market area, competitive equilibrium is established, and the retailers' market area shape is hexagon.

First, suppose that the Lösch competition style prevails among the retailers. Thus, the Lösch competitive equilibrium is established in a market space. In this competitive equilibrium, Eqs. (3.1) and (3.2) should be established:

$$Y = (p - k)Q - F = 0 \tag{3.1}$$

$$\mathrm{d}Y/\mathrm{d}p = (p - k)\mathrm{d}Q/\mathrm{d}p + Q = 0 \tag{3.2}$$

Price p^* and the radius of the inscribed circle of the market area U^* in a Lösch competitive equilibrium can be derived by solving the simultaneous Eqs. (3.1) and (3.2) in the following way. First, the equilibrium price is derived from Eq. (3.1) as a function of U as Eq. (3.3):

T. Ishikawa, *Dynamic Locational Phases of Economic Activity in the Globalized World*, DOI 10.1007/978-981-10-0524-4_3

$$p^{*} = 0.5(a + k - 2 \cdot 3^{0.5}\ 0.2027tU) \tag{3.3}$$

Substituting Eq. (3.3) into p in Eq. (3.2) gives Eq. (3.4):

$$U(a - k - 2 \cdot 3^{05}\ 0.2027tU) - (2 \cdot 3^{0.5}F/3)^{0.5} = 0 \tag{3.4}$$

Second, by solving Eq. (3.4) with respect to U, the equilibrium radius in Lösch competition, U^{*}, can be derived. This is a way to obtain the competitive equilibrium price and the market area size in a Lösch model. Equation (3.4) is used as the key equation to show the correspondence of the Lösch equilibrium to the starting point of the CPC in Sect. 3.2.2.

3.1.2 *Derivation of the Greenhut-Ohta Equilibrium in a Spatial Free-Entry Market Space*

In the original Greenhut-Ohta model, as mentioned previously, the analysis used the delivered price p_v at an apex of the retailer's market area. The variable p_v consists of the price at the retailer's store and the transportation cost of the goods from the retailer to an apex of its market area. Thus, the delivered price, p_v, is given by the function of the price and the radius of the inscribed circle of the market area as Eq. (3.5):

$$p_v = p + \left(2/3^{0.5}\right)tU \tag{3.5}$$

Using p_v, and the radius of the inscribed circle of the market area, the retailer's profit in the Greenhut-Ohta model is represented by Eq. (3.6):

$$\begin{aligned} Y = &-1.8101U^{4} + 12t\,(0.4639p_v - \mathrm{a}/3 - 0.1306k)U^{3} \\ &+ 2 \cdot 3^{0.5}(a - ak - p_v - k)\,p_v U^{2} - F \end{aligned} \tag{3.6}$$

The two equilibrium conditions in the Greenhut-Ohta model are indicated by Eqs. (3.7) and (3.8):

$$Y = 0 \tag{3.7}$$

$$\begin{aligned} \mathrm{d}Y/\mathrm{d}U = &-7.2404U^{3} + 36(0.4639p_v - a/3 - 0.1306k) \\ &+ 4 \cdot 3^{0.5}(a - ak - p_v - k)U = 0 \end{aligned} \tag{3.8}$$

The equilibrium price and the radius of the inscribed circle of the market area are derived as follows. First, from Eq. (3.7), the equilibrium delivered price at an apex of the retailer's market area is given as a function U as Eq. (3.9).

$$p_v^* = 0.5\left(a + 1.6072tU + k - \left((a - 0.7022tU - k)^2 - 2F/(3^{0.5}U^2)\right)^{0.5}\right) \tag{3.9}$$

Second, substituting p_v in Eq. (3.8) with (3.9) gives Eq. (3.10):

$$-0.1233t^2U^2 + 0.1755(a - k)tU + 0.4018UB^{0.5} - F/(2 \cdot 3^{0.5}U^2) = 0 \tag{3.10}$$

where B is $(a - 0.1022tU - k)^2 - 2F / (3^{0.5}U^2)$. The equilibrium radius of the inscribed circle of the market area in the Greenhut-Ohta model is derived by solving Eq. (3.10) with respect to U. This is a way to obtain the equilibrium price and the market area size in a Greenhut-Ohta competition model. Equation (3.10) is used as the key equation to show the correspondence of the Greenhut-Ohta equilibrium to the lowest point of the CPC in Sect. 3.2.2.

3.2 Analysis of Spatial Free-Entry Equilibria Using the Contact Price Curve

3.2.1 *Derivation of the Contact Price Curve*

As mentioned previously, the contact price means the delivered price at the apex of the retailer's market area at which the delivered prices of the rival retailers are contacted and the competition between the retailers is realized. Every apex is the site where the delivered prices of the rival retailers are contacted. The CPC consists of the price p^* in a free-entry competitive equilibrium and the transportation cost of the goods from the retailer to an apex of its market area. The CPC is almost the same as the margin line and frontier price curve (FPC), which was devised by Hoover (1937, 1970). The difference between the CPC and FPC is that the concept of the contact price is emphasized as being determined by the competition between the surrounding rivals.

Now, the contact price (CP) is given by Eq. (3.11)[1]:

$$\text{CP} = p^* + 2/3^{0.5}tU \tag{3.11}$$

The price p^* in Eq. (3.11) is the competitive equilibrium price. Thus, it is obtained from Eq. (3.7). The price p^* in Eq. (3.11) is given by Eq. (3.12):

[1]When retailers have a triangle or square market shape, this assumption becomes a crucial in deriving a competitive equilibrium by using the conjectural variation of price.

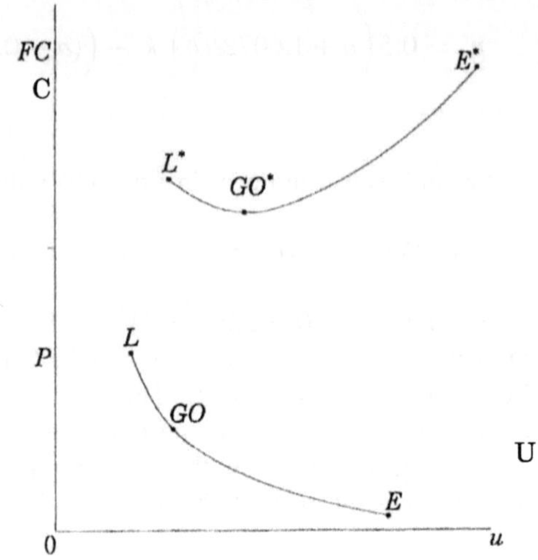

Fig. 3.1 Derivation of the contact price curve

$$p^* = 0.5((a - 2 \cdot 3^{0.5}\, 0.2027tU + k) - ((a - 2 \cdot 3^{0.5}\, 0.2027tU + k)^2 - 4(ak - 2 \cdot 3^{0.5}\, 0.2027tk + 23^{0.5}F/12U^2))^{0.5}) \tag{3.12}$$

The CPC is represented as Eq. (3.13) by adding the transportation cost of goods from the retailer to an apex of its market area to the free-entry competitive price:

$$\mathrm{CPC} = 0.5(a + 1.6072tU + k - ((a - 2 \cdot 3^{0.5}\, 0.2027tU - k)^2 - 2 \cdot 3^{0.5}F/3U^2)^{0.5}) \tag{3.13}$$

To illustrate the CPC as a function of the radius U of the inscribed circle of the market area, numerical values are assigned to marginal and fixed costs as $k = 0$, $F = 0.05a^4$. Then, a CPC is described as the curve of $L^* - GO^* - E^*$ in Fig. 3.1. The *L–GO–E* curve in Fig. 3.1 indicates only the competitive equilibrium prices when the equilibrium radius of the inscribed circle of the market area is expanded.

3.2.2 *Analysis of Free-Entry Competitive Equilibria in a Plane Market Space*

Let us verify the correspondence of the Lösch equilibrium to point L^* of the CPC. The price p^* indicated by point L^* of the CPC means the highest price at retailer's store; thus, the price is equal to the price P_M set by the retailer in the position of monopoly.[2] The price P_M is given by Eq. (3.14).

$$P_M = 0.5(a - 1.6072tU + k) \tag{3.14}$$

Because $p*$ is equal to $P_{M,}$ the term of the square in Eq. (3.13) must be zero. Therefore, the radius U of the inscribed circle of the market area must be satisfied by Eq. (3.15):

$$U(a - k - 2 \cdot 3^{0.5}\, 0.2027tU) - (2 \cdot 3^{0.5} F/3)^{0.5} = 0 \tag{3.15}$$

Equation (3.15) is the same as Eq. (3.4), which is used to obtain the equilibrium radius of the inscribed circle of the market area when the retailers are under Lösch competition. It is said from this fact that the starting point $L*$ of the CPC corresponds to the Lösch competitive equilibrium.

Subsequently, let us examine the correspondence of the Greenhu-Ohta equilibrium to point $GO*$ of the CPC. Point $GO*$ is the lowest point of the CPC. The lowest point $GO*$ of the CPC is derived by differentiating Eq. (3.13) with respect to U and setting it to zero. Thus, by solving Eq. (3.16), the radius of the inscribed circle of the market area is obtained:

$$1.6072tB^{0.5} + 23^{0.5}\, 0.2027tU\left(a - 23^{0.5}\, 0.2027tU - k\right) - 2F/3^{0.5}U^2)) = 0 \tag{3.16}$$

Equation (3.16) is transformed as Eq. (3.17):

$$-0.1233t^2\, U^2 + 0.1755(a - k)tU + 0.4018UB^{0.5} - F/(2 \cdot 3^{0.5}U^2) = 0 \tag{3.17}$$

where $B = (a - 0.1022tU - k)^2 - 2F/\left(3^{0.5}U^2\right)$. Equation (3.17) is the same as Eq. (3.10), which is used to derive the Greenhut-Ohta equilibrium. Consequently, it is clarified that the lowest point of the CPC corresponds to the Greenhut-Ohta competitive equilibrium.

It is said that the CPC is useful for deriving all of the free-entry equilibrium values in certain conditions. In addition, the CPC can indicate the characteristics of the Lösch and the Greenhut-Ohta equilibrium in a simple way.[3] Moreover, as will be shown in Part 3, the CPC enriches the construction methods for establishing city systems by using many retailers' market areas. The city system theory that uses the concept of the CPC easily constructs the city systems with more diversity and explains successfully city systems in the real world.

---

[2]This fact is refereed by Hoover' analysis of the frontier price curve (Hoover 1970, p. 272).

[3]The usefulness of the CPC is demonstrated when a linear market is assumed in the analysis.

Part II
Location Theory of Manufacturing Industry

Chapter 4
Change of a Factory's Production in Agglomeration

4.1 Formation of Industrial Agglomeration

According to the location theory established by Weber (1909), three general location factors decisively influence firm's location determination: transportation cost, labor cost, and agglomeration economies. Therefore, when a firm plans to build a factory and to determine its location, the firm has to pay attention to at least these three factors. An administration that wants to attract factories to its territory also considers these factors to be fundamental elements in its location policy. As transportation systems develop in many countries, the significance of agglomeration economies becomes stronger between these location factors and industrial agglomerations are intentionally constructed in regions. Many regional governments have attracted various factories to their territories by putting agglomeration economies at the center of the location policy. For instance, one of the location strategies is that a regional government builds an industrial park in its territory and prepares a series of subsidies and tax exemptions to attract factories outside the regions. As a result, a kind of an incidental agglomeration is formed in its territory. Even if an agglomeration forms incidentally, the agglomeration economies become generated in the territory. Because the agglomeration economy is the general location factor, all firms naturally pay attention to the territory as a potential location where an agglomeration is established. Based on the generated agglomeration economies, more factories are expected to be attracted to the territory.

Although the economic importance of industrial agglomerations remains at a high level these days, the contents of agglomerations are changed due to economic globalization. This chapter first considers the change of a factory's production mode in an agglomeration by analyzing the relationship between the number of factories and agglomeration economies. Second, the possibility of the fragmentation of factories' production processes is examined from the viewpoint of a factory's production method. This section tries to explain the mechanism of change for the structural production activity in an agglomeration.

T. Ishikawa, *Dynamic Locational Phases of Economic Activity in the Globalized World*, DOI 10.1007/978-981-10-0524-4_4

4.2 The Relationship Between the Number of Factories and Agglomeration Economies

In the period that the demand quantity for the goods of an industry is large, the number of factories in the industry tends to increase; also, the industry tends to locate the factories in a place within an agglomeration in order to produce as much goods as possible. The industry's production mode is organized to achieve more production volume by utilizing internal and external economies in an agglomeration. There may be a relationship between agglomeration economies, the firm's production amount, and the number of the factories in an agglomeration.[1]

4.2.1 *Internal and External Economies in an Agglomeration*

A factory that produces goods in an agglomeration usually enjoys internal economy. The internal economy varies according to the level of the production quantity of the factory. This economy, A_I, is expressed by a function of factory's production quantity, Q, as Eq. (4.1):

$$A_I = -aQ^2 + bQ - C \tag{4.1}$$

where a, b, and C are parameters. The factory also enjoys localization economies, A_E, which arise from accumulation of the production volume in the agglomeration. These economies can be related to the factories' production quantity and the number of factories, N, as shown by Eq. (4.2):

$$A_E = -\alpha\left(\sum_{i=1}^{N} Q_i\right)^2 + \beta\left(\sum_{i=1}^{N} Q_i\right) - D \tag{4.2}$$

where α, β, and D are parameters. Factories located at an agglomeration enjoy two kinds of economies. It is assumed that even if the number of factories is one, the factory enjoys part of the localization economies because the production quantity at the site is increased by the factory's production. If agglomeration economies are negative, it implies that the manufacturing efficiency of a factory gets worse. An agglomeration economy as a whole, A_T, is obtained by summing the internal and external economies as Eq. (4.3):

[1]The framework of the analysis was built by Ishikawa (2015a).

$$A_T = -aQ_i^2 + bQ_i - C + \left(-\alpha\left(\sum_{i=1}^{N} Q_i\right)^2 + \beta\left(\sum_{i=1}^{N} Q_i\right) - D\right) \tag{4.3}$$

Using Eq. (4.3), a factory's quantity, Q^*, that maximizes agglomeration economies is derived as Eq. (4.4):

$$Q^* = (b + \beta N)/(2(a + \alpha N^2)) \tag{4.4}$$

Equation (4.4) indicates that the factory's production quantity that maximizes agglomeration economies varies as the number of factories in the agglomeration increases.

Let us analyze the relationships between agglomeration economies, the firm's production amount, and the number of factories in an agglomeration by assigning numerical values to the parameters as shown in Table 4.1.

Figure 4.1 shows that the factory's production quantity that maximizes agglomeration economies varies according to the number of the factories at an agglomeration.

4.2.2 *Relationship Between the Number of Factories and Agglomeration Economies*

The agglomeration economy enjoyed by a factory is represented as a function of the number of the factories as Eq. (4.5). Figure 4.2 shows agglomeration economies as a function of the number of the factories in an agglomeration.

Table 4.1 Values of the parameters

a	b	C	D	α	β
0.04	4	20	53.3	0.0008	0.73

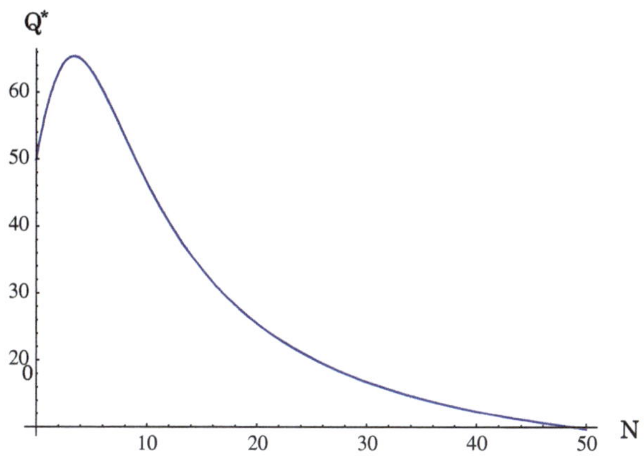

Fig. 4.1 Relationship between a factory's production quantity and the number of factories

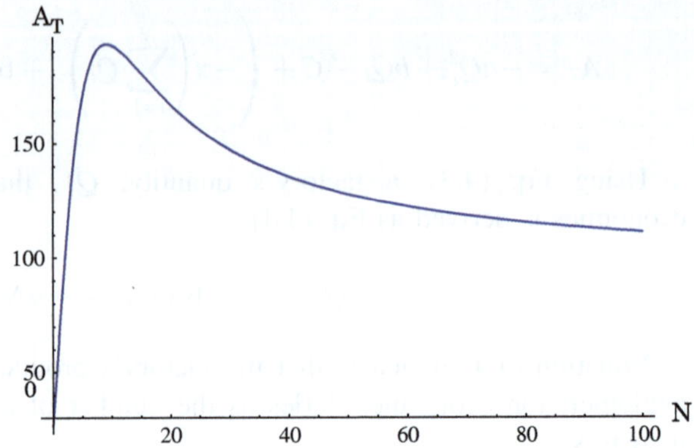

Fig. 4.2 Agglomeration economies in agglomeration as a function of the number of factories

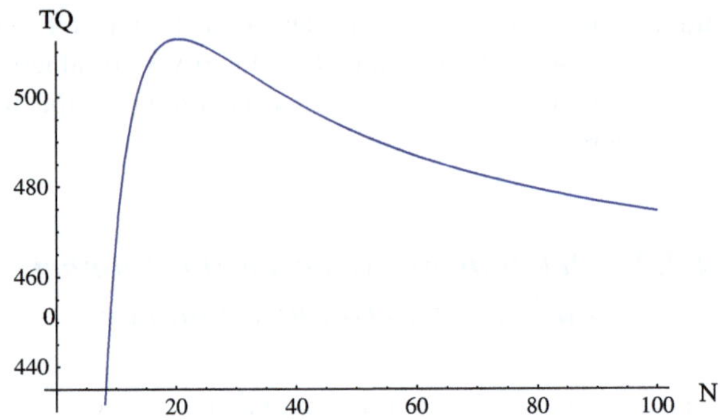

Fig. 4.3 Variation of total production quantity as the number of factories increase

$$\begin{aligned} A_T = &\left(-a * ((\beta N + b)/(2(a + \alpha N^2)))^2 + b((\beta N + b)/(2(a + \alpha N^2))) - C\right) \\ &+ \left(-\alpha(N * ((\beta N + b)/(2(a + \alpha N^2))))^2 + \beta(N * ((\beta N + b)/(2(a + \alpha N^2)))) - D\right) \end{aligned} \tag{4.5}$$

The total production quantity in the agglomeration changes as the number of the factories increases. The quantity is indicated by Eq. (4.6):

$$TQ = ((b + \beta N)/(2(a + \alpha N^2)))N \tag{4.6}$$

The total production quantity in the agglomeration is depicted as a function of the number of firms in an agglomeration, as shown in Fig. 4.3. The production quantity in the agglomeration decreases after the number of the factories goes beyond a certain number of factories in agglomeration.

The above equations clarify that the number of the factories to maximize the total production quantity in an agglomeration is larger than that to maximize the agglomeration economies. These numbers of factories are shown in Table 4.2.

Table 4.2 Number of factories that maximize agglomeration economies and production

Number of factories that maximize of agglomeration economies	9.13
Number of factories that maximize of total production amounts	20.67

4.2.3 Mechanism of Structural Changes of Production in Agglomeration

A factory's production is assumed implicitly in the agglomeration analysis in those days that a factory processes the raw materials to the finished goods in one production plant. For example, a factory's production processes are assumed to be as illustrated in Fig. 4.4: three factories A, B, and C co-exist at an agglomeration, and each factory has four processes (I, II, III, and IV) in its plant to produce the final goods.

Let us consider changes to the factory's production mode in an agglomeration, assuming that each production process has different characteristics: process I produces basic material goods from the raw material by using large machines; process II makes a lot of parts of the final goods from the basic material goods by using many laborers; process III produces semifinal goods by using much electronic energy; and process IV makes the finished goods from the intermediate goods by using skilled workers. In the period that logistics and communication technologies are not developed, these four processes are concentrated in a factory at an agglomeration to curb the overhead costs necessary to connect the works of the four processes.

The firms within the agglomeration may notice that they can reduce production costs by outsourcing the production of basic material goods to a new established firm D, which produces only material goods by utilizing the larger machines. The three firms A, B, and C can obtain the basic material goods at lower costs from the new firm D, which enjoys scale economies due to operating a large apparatus; also, each of the three firms starts to utilize a larger production space that was occupied by process I. This is the starting point of the division of labor in an agglomeration. If the division of labor in an agglomeration proceeds, each firm specializes in a process to complete the final goods with lower production costs. Figure 4.5

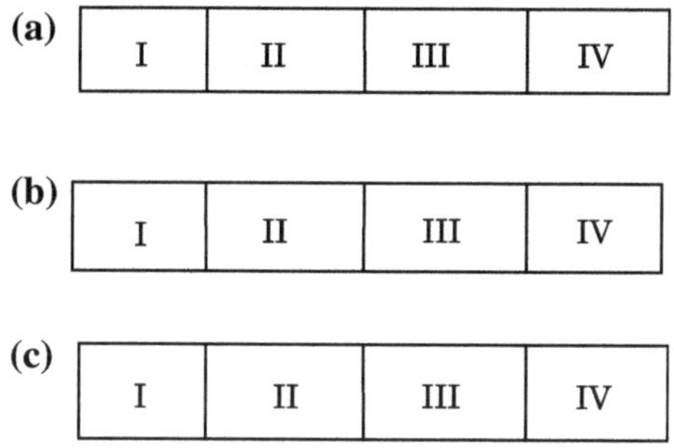

Fig. 4.4 Four production processes of each factory in an agglomeration

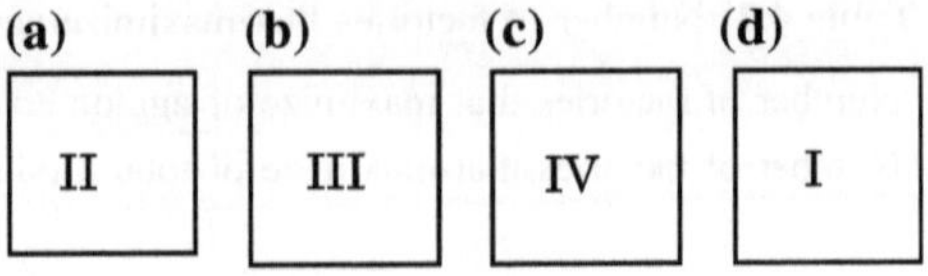

Fig. 4.5 Change of production structure in agglomeration

illustrates this production situation. It is said that the final goods are produced not by individual firms but by a community in which agglomeration is formed.

The change of the production mode in agglomerations is generated by the interlocking of two kinds of economies—the internal and external economies. As the interlock of the two kinds of economies deepens, the fragmentation of the production process largely develops. The original production mode in agglomeration does not remain; it is diversified not only horizontally and but also vertically by the two kinds of agglomeration economies.[2]

4.2.4 *Reformation of Agglomerations Due to Fragmentation Production*

The fragmentation of firms' production processes makes the production structure in agglomeration unstable. Fragmentation makes individual production processes small and simple. Each process becomes so simple that every worker is able to easily understand the content of the process. Workers are not required to undergo long-term training to take part in the assigned process; thus, their wage rates are curbed to low levels. In addition, because the production content is simple, machineries are easily installed into the process. Small and simple production processes tend to be easily moved over long distances; they are easily shifted to places where the required infrastructure is equipped and labor costs are relatively low. Some production processes remain in the existing agglomerations; they need unique skills that exist in the existing agglomerations. As a result, the production systems of the manufacturing firms in the existing agglomerations expand beyond the area of the agglomeration, and all production factories are combined by the various network systems in terms of logistics, finances, and information.

It is possible to elucidate the change of the production structure in agglomeration from the viewpoint of a network system. The network systems of logistics, finances, and communications support the movement of various production processes from the existing agglomerations to the places that provide circumstances suitable to the production processes. If the functions that operate the network system in the existing agglomerations would not be adequately developed, a firm's production processes could not be spatially divided. Because the original network system is

[2]From the viewpoint of history, Lazonick (1986) explained the change of the production structure of the textile industry in England.

generated by the division of labor at the early stage of the formation of the agglomeration, it is said that the mechanism that makes the production structure in agglomeration unstable was embedded since the starting point of the formation of agglomerations.

4.3 Spatial Departure of Production Processes from Agglomeration

This section analyzes how a firm fragments its production processes and what factors affect the firm's fragmenting processes. It then examines how laborers are allocated between the production processes of the firm.

4.3.1 Assumptions for the Analysis of a Factory's Production Function

To proceed with the analysis of the fragmentation of production processes, the following assumptions are set. The market of the final goods produced by the manufacturing firm is competitive and the price of the goods in the marketplace is given to the firm. The production costs that the firm can spend to produce the finished goods are given to the firm. The firm thus manages its production processes to maximize its profit under the given good's price and production costs.

The production function of the firm is given by Eq. (4.7)[3]:

$$Q = (x^{\sigma} + y^{\sigma})^{\theta/\sigma} L_q^{a(1-\theta)} \tag{4.7}$$

Here, Q is the production quantity of the final goods; x and y are two kinds of the intermediate goods (they also reveal the quantities used to produce the final goods); L_q is the number of laborers used to make the finished goods in the final stage of the production processes; and σ, θ, and a are parameters. Parameter σ is related to the economy of the diversity and parameter a is related to the economy of the specialty; they are assumed to be $0 < \sigma < 1$, and $a > 0$. Increasing the economy of the diversity is represented by a decrease of the value of σ. Increasing the economy of the specialization is represented by the increase of the value of a. The parameter θ is assumed to be $\theta < 1$.

[3]Shi and Yang (1995) analyzes the fragmentation of production processes and the allocation of labors between production processes by using the similar production function. Dluhosch (2000) clearly explains the logic of the spatial distribution of production process. Arndt and Kierzkowski (2001) introduces the fragmentation of production from the various ways.

The intermediate goods y are produced by laborers L_y as shown by Eq. (4.8):

$$y = L_y^a \tag{4.8}$$

Intermediate goods x are produced as indicated by Eqs. (4.9) and (4.10). The intermediate goods x are made by goods w and labor L_x as shown by Eq. (4.9). Goods w are produced by labor L_w as represented by Eq. (4.10):

$$x = w^{\theta} L_x^{a(1-\theta)} \tag{4.9}$$

$$w = L_w^a \tag{4.10}$$

Three kinds of the firm's production modes are assumed:

1. *Simple production mode in a factory*: The final goods are produced by using the intermediate goods y and labor L_y and L_q in one factory.
2. *The full division production mode in a factory*: Two intermediate goods y and x are used, and the four kinds of labors are employed to produce the final goods within a factory.
3. *Spatially fragmented production mode*: The final goods are produced by using the four kinds of laborers in the production processes, which are spatially separated from each other.

4.3.2 A Firm's Profits as Derived from Different Production Modes

4.3.2.1 A Firm's Profit from a Simple Production Mode

Let us derive a firm's profit, Y_1, when the firm selects a simple production mode in a factory. When the firm selects this mode, the firm's profit is represented as Eq. (4.11):

$$Y_1 = p(L_y^{a\sigma})^{\theta/\sigma} L_q^{a(1-\theta)} - w_q L_q - w_y L_y \tag{4.11}$$

Here, w_q and w_y are wage rates of labor L_q and L_y, respectively. If the production cost is given as C, the firm determines the numbers for two kinds of labor using Eq. (4.12):

$$Y_1 = p(L_y^{a\sigma})^{\theta/\sigma} L_q^{a(1-\theta)} - w_q L_q - w_y L_y + \lambda(\bar{C} - w_q L_q - w_y L_y) \tag{4.12}$$

The optimal numbers of L_q and L_y are obtained by differentiating Eq. (4.12) by L_q and L_y, respectively. The number of each kind of laborer is indicated by Eqs. (4.13) and (4.14):

$$L_q = ((1-\theta)/w_q)\bar{C} \tag{4.13}$$

$$L_y = (\theta/w_y)\bar{C} \tag{4.14}$$

4.3.2.2 A Firm's Profit Derived from Full Division Production in a Factory

When a firm uses the full division production mode in a factory, the firm determines each kind of worker to maximize its profit, Y_2, by using Eq. (4.15):

$$\begin{aligned} Y_2 = {} & p(L_w^{ao}L_x^{a(1-\theta)\sigma} + L_y^{a\sigma})^{\theta/\sigma}L_q^{a(1-\theta)} - w_qL_q - w_yL_y - w_xL_x - w_wL_w \\ & + \lambda(\bar{C} - w_qL_q - w_yL_y - w_xL_x - w_wL_w) \end{aligned} \tag{4.15}$$

where w_x and w_w are wage rates of labor L_x and L_w, respectively. In this case, the numbers of four kinds of laborers are derived by Eq. (4.16a–d):

$$L_w = (w_x/w_w)(\theta/(1-\theta))L_x \tag{4.16a}$$

$$L_y = (w_y w_x^{a\sigma\theta-1}/w_w^{a\sigma\theta})^{1/(a\sigma-1)}\,(\theta^{a\sigma\theta}(1-\theta)^{1-a\theta\sigma})^{1/(a\sigma-1)}L_x \tag{4.16b}$$

$$L_q = ((w_y/w_q)((1-\theta)/\theta)(((w_x/w_w)\theta/(1-\theta))^{a\sigma\theta} + E^{a\sigma})/E^{a\sigma-1})L_x \tag{4.16c}$$

E is shown as follows:

$$\begin{aligned} & E:(w_y w_x^{a\sigma\theta-1}/w_w^{a\sigma\theta})^{1/(a\sigma-1)}\,(\theta^{a\sigma\theta}(1-\theta)^{1-a\theta\sigma})^{1/(a\sigma-1)} \\ & L_x = (1/(w_qM + w_yR + w_x + w_wN)\bar{C} \end{aligned} \tag{4.16d}$$

M, R, and N in the above equations are shown as follows:

$$\begin{aligned} & M:(w_y/w_q)((1-\theta)/\theta)(((w_x/w_w)\theta/(1-\theta))^{a\sigma\theta} + E^{a\sigma})/E^{a\sigma-1} \\ & R:(w_y w_x^{a\sigma\theta-1}/w_w^{a\sigma\theta})^{1/(a\sigma-1)}\,(\theta^{a\sigma\theta}(1-\theta)^{1-a\theta\sigma})^{1/(a\sigma-1)} \\ & N:(w_x/w_w)(\theta/(1-\theta)) \end{aligned}$$

4.3.2.3 A Firm's Profit Derived from Spatially Fragmented Production Mode

Let us derive the firm's profit, $Y_{3,}$ when the firm selects a spatially fragmented production mode. In this case, the firm locates the final production process in the home country and scatters other processes over foreign countries to take advantage of low wage rates in other countries, even if locating factories in foreign countries incurs the transportation costs of the intermediate goods. It is assumed in this analysis that intermediate goods y and x are produced in country x and y; the distances between each factory are the same, D; and the freight rates of the intermediate goods y, x, and w are shown by t_y, t_x, and $t_{w.}$ The wage rates of three countries y, x, and w are denoted by $w_{yf,}$ w_{xf}, and $w_{wf,}$ respectively. The wage rate of the home country is w_q.

Using the next Eq. (4.17), the firm determines the number of laborers of each production process according to the Eq. (4.18a–e):

$$\begin{aligned}Y_3 = p(L_w^{ao}L_x^{a(1-\theta)\sigma} + L_y^{a\sigma})^{\theta/\sigma}L_q^{a(1-\theta)} - w_qL_q - w_{yf}L_y - w_{xf}L_x - w_{wf}L_w - t_yL_y^aD - t_xL_w^{a\theta}L_x^{a(1-\theta)}D - t_wL_w^aD\\ \lambda(\bar{C} - w_qL_q - w_{yf}L_y - w_{xf}L_x - w_{wf}L_w - t_yL_y^aD - t_xL_w^{a\theta}L_x^{a(1-\theta)}D - t_wL_w^aD)\end{aligned} \tag{4.17}$$

Because the derivation of the numbers of the four kinds of laborers are cumbersome, a numerical calculation is introduced. The numbers of the four types of laborers are determined by solving simultaneous equation systems (4.18a–e) with respect to L_q, L_{yf}, L_{xf}, L_{wf}, and λ, respectively.

$$\partial Y_3/\partial L_q = 0 \tag{4.18a}$$

$$\partial Y_3/\partial L_{yf} = 0 \tag{4.18b}$$

$$\partial Y_3/\partial L_{xf} = 0 \tag{4.18c}$$

$$\partial Y_3/\partial L_{wf} = 0 \tag{4.18d}$$

$$\partial Y_3/\partial \lambda = 0 \tag{4.18e}$$

4.3.2.4 The Relationships Between Production Modes and Firm's Profits

Let us compare the firm's profits that are obtained for the three kinds of the production modes, assigning the following numerical values to the parameters: $p = 20$, $w_q = 1.5$, $w_y = 1.2$, $w_x = 1.6$, $w_w = 1.4$, $w_{yf} = 0.6$, $w_{xf} = 1.2$, $w_{wf} = 0.7$, $D = 2.5$, $t_y = 0.1$, $t_x = 0.2$, $t_w = 0.1$, and $\theta = 0.5$. The value of parameter a is assumed to be 0.7, which indicates the economy of the specialization; the value of σ is 0.45, which reveals the economy of the diversity.

Table 4.3 The firm's profits and allocation of labor (*a* = 0.7, σ = 0.45)

Mode	Y	Q	L_q	L_y	L_x	L_w
(1)	184.4	16.72	62.5	50.0	*na*	*na*
(2)	341.0	24.55	50.0	37.72	9.29	10.61
(3)	430.4	29.0	48.84	71.07	10.43	16.83

Table 4.3 shows the firm's profits derived for the three kinds of production modes. The firm's profit is the highest as the firm selects the spatially fragmented production mode. It is known from the comparison of the firm's profits indicated in Table 4.3 that the firm increases its profit by shifting the factories that produce the intermediate goods to the foreign countries.

Changing the value of parameter a from 0.6 to 0.8, 1.2, and 1.4, the firm's profit is derived against each value of a. The effects of economy of the specialization of the firm's production activity can be examined. Table 4.4 shows the effects of economy of the specialization on the firm. As shown by Table 4.4, as the economy of the specialization becomes higher, the firm's profit and production quantity increase in every production mode. When a is lower than 1.2, the firm's profit and the production quantity obtained by the spatially fragmented production mode are the highest. When a is 1.4, the firm's profit and production amount are the highest when the firm selects the full division production mode in a factory.

Subsequently, let us analyze the effects of the economy of the diversity on the firm's production activities. In this analysis, the value of a is fixed at 0.7, and the value of the parameter σ is assumed to be 0.25 and 0.55. Table 4.5 indicates the firm's profits derived for the three kinds of production modes. In both cases of the values of 0.25 and 0.55, the firm's profit is the highest when the mode of the spatial full fragmentation is

Table 4.4 Increase of economies of specialization and firm's production activity

Mode	Y	Q	L_q	L_y	L_x	L_w
a = 0.6, σ = 0.45						
(1)	73.60	11.18	62.5	50.0	*na*	*na*
(2)	196.0	17.3	50.0	36.48	9.75	11.15
(3)	253.4	20.17	48.92	70.67	11.47	18.95
a = 0.8						
(1)	350	25.0	62.5	50.0	*na*	*na*
(2)	547.8	34.89	50.0	39.11	8.77	10.02
(3)	678.8	41.44	48.88	70.20	9.31	14.55
a = 1.2						
(1)	2350	125	62.5	50.0	*na*	*na*
(2)	2755.6	145.28	50.0	46.57	5.97	6.83
(3)	2803.8	147.7	51.62	46.25	4.53	9.04
a = 1.4						
(1)	5540.2	279.51	62.5	50.0	*na*	*na*
(2)	5897.0	302.39	50.0	51.61	4.08	4.67
(3)	4879.1	251.46	54.53	30.73	5.43	6.01

Table 4.5 Increase of economies of diversity and the firm's production activity

Mode	Y	Q	L_q	L_y	L_x	L_w
$\sigma = 0.55$, $a = 0.7$						
(1)	184.4	16.72	62.5	50.0	*na*	*na*
(2)	279.4	21.47	50.0	39.95	8.45	9.66
(3)	359.4	25.47	48.88	76.23	9.16	14.76
$\sigma = 0.25$						
(1)	184.4	16.72	62.5	50.0	*na*	*na*
(2)	751.2	45.06	50.0	34.27	10.58	12.10
(3)	909.3	52.96	48.80	63.04	12.40	20.08

Table 4.6 Effects of freight rates of intermediate goods on the firm's production activities

Mode	Y	Q	L_q	L_y	L_x	L_w
$\sigma = 0.55$, $a = 0.7$						
Freight rate, $t_y = 0.8$, $t_x = 1$, $t_w = 0.8$						
(3)	254.8	20.24	45.43	44.61	6.40	5.36

selected by the manufacturing firm. It is known from the comparison of the firm's profits shown in Table 4.5 that the firm increases its profit by shifting the factories that produce the intermediate goods to the foreign countries as the economy of the diversity increases. When the mode of simple production is used by the firm, the allocation of laborers does not change even if the economy of the diversity increases.

Lastly, let us examine the effects of the freight rates of the intermediate goods between the factories when the firm selects the spatially fragmented production mode by increasing the values of t_y, t_x, and t_w to 0.8, 1.0, and 0.8, respectively. In this case, the firm's profit, production amount, and number of each kind of laborer are shown in Table 4.6, where a is 0.7 and σ is 0.55. As the freight rates increase, the firm's profit and production amount decrease; they are less than those of the full division production mode in a factory.

The above analysis shows that if the economies of the specialty and diversity increase and the freight rates decrease according to the progress of the technology of production and transportation, the firm's production processes are likely to be fragmented. The fragmented production blocs are spatially scattered to reduce the production costs.

Chapter 5
Location Theory for a Factory in the Globalized World

This chapter analyzes how manufacturing firms find out the locations of fragmented production blocs separate from existing agglomerations. In addition, this chapter proposes a method for a firm to determine the location of a new factory in a fragmented production bloc for manufacturing intermediate goods in a large geographical space.

5.1 Factory's Location in the Globalized World

It would not take a long time for a firm to determine a location for its factory when the firm's activities are basically confined to one country. In the globalized economy, a firm undertakes a series of processes to decide its factory's location because the spatial range of the firm's activity is expanded to a large area of several countries. In this case, a firm faces the issue of country selection and site choices within the selected country. To decide a factory's location, a firm proceeds with the location determination processes step by step, deliberating various location factors. In particular, corporate tax and interest rates are important location factors in the early stages of the location determination process because these factors decisively affect the firm's regional choices as well as country selections.

In the globalized economy, a new mechanism begins to work in the firm's production management: the function of the transfer price of intermediate goods. Many manufacturing firms fragment the production process into several blocs and scatter the fragmented blocs across countries. Thus, the intermediate goods produced by each factory are moved between the factories, which are located in different countries. In the movement of the intermediate goods, the transfer price is utilized.[1] The firm can measure each factory's profit by using the transfer price and

[1]The transfer price has been extensively studied by Hirshleifer (1956) and Eden (1985).

T. Ishikawa, *Dynamic Locational Phases of Economic Activity in the Globalized World*, DOI 10.1007/978-981-10-0524-4_5

estimating each factory's contribution to the firm. The function of the transfer price is important in the management of the firm's activity. The same thing applies to the governments of the countries, because the country in which factories are located can charge corporate tax on the factory's profit, which is grasped by the transfer price. In the global economy, the location power of the corporate tax rate and the interest rate, which did not fully exercise location power in the pro-global era, should be accurately examined. The location factor and the function of the transfer price require further investigation by researchers.

The primary purpose of this chapter is to clearly show the location power of the corporation tax rate and the interest rate through the function of the transfer price. To clearly verify that the corporation tax and the interest rate have the power to shift the factory's location, it is appropriate to analyze their locational power in a specified model and show how they change the factory's location in a large geographical space. To this end, this chapter constructs a simple location determination model based on the traditional location theory and uses a simulation method. Based on the constructed model, the chapter first analyzes the location power of the corporate tax rate, which is determined by the government. Second, the interest rate, which is manipulated the central bank, is incorporated into the model, and the location power of the interest rate is examined. In these examinations, the gradient dynamics method is adopted; this method, by generating a chaotic phenomenon on the three-dimensional sphere, can provide useful information about the firm's location determination process in a large geographical space.[2]

5.2 Derivation of the Profit Function of a Firm

5.2.1 Assumptions and Framework of the Analysis

To analyze the location power of the corporate tax rate and the interest rate, this section introduces the assumptions and framework according to the traditional location theory.[3]

A firm produces the finished goods by using two production processes. The first process is conducted by factory 1, which is in the home country. Factory 1 manufactures intermediate goods, mq. The second process is assigned to factory 2, which is located in a foreign country. Factory 2 composes the final goods by using the intermediate goods.

---

[2]Puu (1998) used gradient dynamics to analyze the factory's location in two dimensions. This chapter uses the same gradient dynamics in three dimensions.

[3]The basic framework is constructed according to Weber (1909), Puu (1998) and Ishikawa (2009, 2015b).

The intermediate goods produced by factory 1 are transported to factory 2 by the transfer price *mp*. Factory 2 uses one unit of the intermediate goods to produce one unit of final goods. Factory 2 sells the finished goods to the marketplace in the foreign country. There is no tariff in the movement of the intermediate goods between the two factories.

Factory 2 is in the position of the monopoly in the market. Thus, factory 2 can determines the supply quantity of the final goods in the market. This factory decides the quantity in order to maximize the *factory's* profit. On the other hand, factory 1 decides the transfer price of the intermediate goods in order to maximize the *firm's* profits.

The corporate tax rates of the home and the foreign country are represented by t and t^*, respectively. The interest rates of the home and the foreign country are indicated by r and r^*. At the first stage of the analysis, the interest rates are not considered for simplification. The effects of the interest rates will be examined in the second stage of the analysis.

5.2.2 Derivation of the Profit Function of Factory 1

The profit of the factory 1, Y_1, is given by Eq. (5.1):

$$Y_1 = (1-t)[mp * mq - C(mq) - F_1] \tag{5.1}$$

where $C(mq)$ is the cost function of factory 1 and F_1 is the fixed cost.

The cost function $C(mq)$ is derived on the basis of the following assumptions. Factory 1 uses two different kinds of materials (m_1, m_2) to produce the intermediate goods. Factory 1 also needs lubricating oil m_3 to operate machines, The materials m_1, m_2, and oil m_3 are produced at points M_1, M_2, and M_3, which are identified by coordinates (x_1, y_1), (x_2, y_2), and (x_3, y_3), respectively. These materials are transported to factory 1 located at point L, which is indicated by (x, y). The freight rates of the materials m_1, m_2 are denoted by t_m, and the freight rate of the oil m_3 is given by t_e. The intermediate goods are transported from factory 1 to factory 2, which is located in the market at point M_4, (x_4, y_4). The freight rate of the intermediate goods is t_g. The mill prices of these materials and oil are assumed to be given for simplicity; these prices are denoted by p_1, p_2, and p_3. Figure 5.1 illustrates the geographical relationship between factory 1, factory 2, the market, and the points of the three materials.

The territory of the home country is shown by the square area in Fig. 5.1. The foreign country is assumed to be rectangular area. The market is indicated by the black square at point M_4 in Fig. 5.1. The border between the two countries is shown by the horizontal bold line in Fig. 5.1.

Fig. 5.1 Location figure

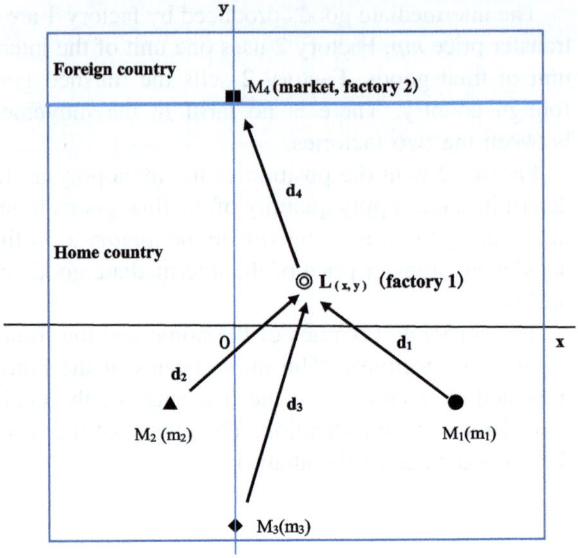

The production function of factory 1 is supposed as Eq. (5.2):

$$mq = Am_1^{\alpha} m_2^{\beta} \tag{5.2}$$

where A, α, and β are parameters and they are defined as $A > 0$ and $0 < (\alpha + \beta) < 1$.

The distances between the material places, M_i (i = 1, 2, 3) and factory 1 are represented by d_1, d_2, and d_3, respectively:

$$d_1 = \left((x - x_1)^2 + (y + y_1)^2\right)^{0.5} \tag{5.3a}$$

$$d_2 = \left((x + x_2)^2 + (y + y_2)^2\right)^{0.5} \tag{5.3b}$$

$$d_3 = \left(x^2 + (y + y_3)^2\right)^{0.5} \tag{5.3c}$$

The distance between factory 1 and factory 2, which is located in the market M_4, is given by d_4:

$$d_4 = \left(x^2 + (y - y_4)^2\right)^{0.5} \tag{5.3d}$$

Thus, the delivered prices P_i ($i = 1, 2, 3$) of the two materials and the lubricating oil at the location of factory 1 are shown by Eqs. (5.4a)–(5.4c), respectively:

$$P_1 = p_1 + t_{\mathrm{m}} d_1 \tag{5.4a}$$

$$P_2 = p_2 + t_{\mathrm{m}} d_2 \tag{5.4b}$$

$$P_3 = p_3 + t_e d_3 \tag{5.4c}$$

The price of the intermediate goods at the location of factory 2, DP, is represented by Eq. (5.5):

$$\mathrm{DP} = mp - t_{\mathrm{g}} d_4 \tag{5.5}$$

Now, making use of the law of equi-marginal productivity (i.e., the ratio between the productivities of the two intermediate goods should be equal to the ratio between the delivered prices of them), the quantities of these materials are derived as Eqs. (5.6a) and (5.6b). (For simplicity, α and β are assumed to be $\alpha = \beta = 0.4$.)

$$m_1 = A^{-1.25} mq^{1.25} ((p_2 + t_{\mathrm{m}} d_2)/(p_1 + t_{\mathrm{m}} d_1))^{0.5} \tag{5.6a}$$

$$m_2 = A^{-1.25} mq^{1.25} ((p_1 + t_{\mathrm{m}} d_1)/(p_2 + t_{\mathrm{m}} d_2))^{0.5} \tag{5.6b}$$

The quantity of oil m_3 is given by a linear function of the amount of the final goods as Eq. (5.6c):

$$m_3 = mq \tag{5.6c}$$

From the above equations, the cost function $C(qm)$ is obtained as Eq. (5.7):

$$C(mq) = 2A^{-1.25} mq^{1.25} (p_1 + t_{\mathrm{m}} d_1)^{0.5} (p_2 + t_{\mathrm{m}} d_2)^{0.5} + mq(p_3 + t_e d_3) + F_1 \tag{5.7}$$

The profit function of factory 1 can be rewritten as Eq. (5.8):

$$Y_1 = (1 - t)\left[mq((mp - t_{\mathrm{g}} d_4) - (p_3 + t_e d_3)) - 2mq^{1.25} A^{-1.25} (p_1 + t_{\mathrm{m}} d_1)^{0.5} (p_2 + t_{\mathrm{m}} d_2)^{0.5} - F_1\right] \tag{5.8}$$

5.2.3 The Profit Functions of Factory 2 and the Firm

Let us derive profit of factory 2. The profit is derived under the following assumptions: The market demand function is represented by Eq. (5.9):

$$p = a - vQ \tag{5.9}$$

where p is the market price of the final goods, a is the maximum reservation price, and v is the parameter. For simplicity, a and v are assumed to be 600 and 1, respectively. If the cost of composing the intermediate goods to the finished goods is represented by $C(Q)$ and fixed cost of factory 2 is represented by F_2, the profit of factory 2, Y_2, is represented by Eq. (5.10):

$$Y_2 = (1 - t^*)[pQ - mp * mq - C(Q) - F_2] \tag{5.10}$$

Suppose that the composing cost $C(Q)$ is given by Eq. (5.11):

$$C(Q) = b\,Q(g + Q)^2/h \tag{5.11}$$

where b, g, and h are parameters that are assumed to be 1.5, 2, and 200 for the simplicity of the calculation, respectively.

Because factory 2 uses one unit of the intermediate goods to produce one final good, mq can be replaced by Q. The profit function is rewritten by Eq. (5.12):

$$Y_2 = (1 - t^*)\left[(p - mp)Q - 1.5\,Q(2 + Q)^2/200 - F_2\right] \tag{5.12}$$

Because the market price of the final good, p, is a function of the quantity Q as shown by Eq. (5.9), the optimal quantity supplied at the market to maximize the profit of factory 2 can be derived by using Eq. (5.12). The optimal supply quantity is given by Eq. (5.13):

$$Q = 0.22(-206 + (582{,}409 - 900mp)^{0.5}) \tag{5.13}$$

As the supply quantity Q is a function of the transfer price, mp, then the profit of factory 2 is also represented as a function of the transfer price as Eq. (5.14):

$$\begin{aligned} Y_2 = (1 - t^*)\Big[\Big(600 - \Big(0.22\Big(-206 + (582{,}409 - 900mp)^{0.5}\Big)\Big) - mp\Big)(0.22(-206 \\ + (582{,}409 - 900mp)^{0.5}\Big)\Big) - F_2\Big]. \end{aligned} \tag{5.14}$$

Eventually, summing up the profits of factory 1 and 2, the firm's profit, Y, can be obtained as Eq. (5.15). The firm's profit is a function of the transfer price, mp, and the location site, (x, y), of factory 1:

$$\begin{aligned}Y = (1-t)\Big[\Big(0.22\Big(-206+(582{,}409-900mp)^{0.5}\Big)\Big)\Big((mp-t_{g}d_{4})-(p_{3}+t_{e}d_{3})\Big)\\ -2\Big(0.22\Big(-206+(582{,}409-900mp)^{0.5}\Big)\Big)^{1.25}A^{-1.25}(p_{1}+t_{m}d_{1})^{0.5}(p_{2}+t_{m}d_{2})^{0.5}-F_{1}\Big]\\ +(1-t^{*})\Big[\Big(600-\Big(0.22\Big(-206+(582{,}409-900mp)^{0.5}\Big)\Big)-mp\Big)\Big(0.22\Big(-206\\ +(582{,}409-900mp)^{0.5}\Big)\Big)-F_{2}\Big].\end{aligned} \tag{5.15}$$

5.3 Settlement of a Prospective Location

5.3.1 Usefulness of a Chaotic Phenomenon

Let us derive the optimal location (*X*, *Y*) of factory 1 and the optimal transfer price by using Eq. (5.15). To derive the optimal transfer price and the location of factory 1, gradient dynamics are used (Puu 1998; Ishikawa 2009). This method is very useful because it can identify the solution point. Furthermore, even if the solution cannot be specified, the sphere in which the solution is included is indicated by a chaotic phenomenon.

The essence of gradient dynamics is that, first, an initial value set is given to x_n, y_n, and mp_n in Eqs. (5.16a)–(5.16c) as a temporal solution. The second tentative values of x_{n+1}, y_{n+1}, and mp_{n+1} are obtained by calculations indicated by the three Eqs. (5.16a)–(5.16c). The same calculation is iterated until a given tentative solution can be approximately judged as the solution. If the values of $(x_{n+1}, y_{n+1}, mp_{n+1})$ in Eqs. (5.16a)–(5.16c) become approximately the same as those of (x_n, y_n, mp_n), the values can be admitted as the solution:

$$x_{n+1} = x_n + j * \partial Y/\partial x, \tag{5.16a}$$

$$y_{n+1} = y_n + j * \partial Y/\partial y, \tag{5.16b}$$

$$mp_{n+1} = mp_n + j * \partial Y/\partial mp, \tag{5.16c}$$

where *j* is the width of a step and *n* shows the number of the calculation. The values of $\partial Y/\partial x$, $\partial Y/\partial y$, and $\partial Y/\partial mp$ are given by Eqs. (5.17a)–(5.17c), where the corporate tax rates of the two countries are assumed to be $t = t^* = 0.82$.

$$\partial Y/\partial x = 0.18\Big[-tgx\,(299.4-0.5mp)/d_4 + (299.4-0.5mp)\big(-t_g(x/d_4) - t_e(x/d_3)\big) - A^{-1.25}(299.4-0.5mp)^{1.25}t_m\Big[\Big\{(p_2+t_m d_2)^{0.5}/(p_1+t_m d_1)^{0.5}\Big\}(x-x_1)/d_1 + \Big\{(p_1+t_m d_1)^{0.5}/(p_2+t_m d_2)^{0.5}\Big\}(x+x_2)/d_2\Big]\Big] = 0 \tag{5.17a}$$

$$\partial Y/\partial y = 0.18\Big[-tg(y-1)(299.4-0.5mp)/d_4 + (299.4-0.5mp)(-t_g((y-y_4)/d_4) - t_e((y-y_3)/d_3) - A^{-1.25}(299.4-0.5mp)^{1.25}t_m\Big[\Big\{(p_2+t_m d_2)^{0.5}/(p_1+t_m d_1)^{0.5}\Big\}(y+y_1)/d_1 + \Big\{(p_1+t_m d_1)^{0.5}/(p_2+t_m d_2)^{0.5}\Big\}(y+y_2)/d_2\Big]\Big] = 0 \tag{5.17b}$$

$$\partial Y/\partial mp = 0.18[-(0.5*mp-299.4)] + 0.22[299.4 - 2*0.5mp + 0.5t_g d_4 + 0.5(p_3+t_e d_3) + 2.5A^{-1.25}(p_2+t_m d_2)^{0.5}(p_1+t_m d_1)^{0.5}(299.4-0.5mp)^{0.25}] = 0. \tag{5.17c}$$

Let us derive the optimal location of factory 1 and the transfer price by assigning numerical values to parameters as follows: (x_1 = 3, y_1 = −0.5), (x_2 = $-3^{0.5}$, y_2 = −0.5), (x_3 = 0, y_3 = −1.5), (x_4 = 0, y_4 = 1), A = 1, p_1 = 0.25, p_2 = 2, p_3 = 0.2, t_m = 0.11, t_e = 0.01, t_g = 0.225, F_1 = 5000, and F_2 = 2500.

The calculation results derived from the gradient dynamics are shown in Fig. 5.2. Figure 5.2 indicates that the optimal transfer price is approximately 442 and the optimal location site is hidden by a chaotic phenomenon.[4] Although the accurate location of factory 1 is not identified by the appearance of a chaotic phenomenon, the chaotic phenomenon provides very important information: the optimal location site is within the area where a chaotic phenomenon appears because the phenomenon appears to surround the optimal solution. If the firm locates factory 1 within the chaotic area, the firm's profit do not vary much.[5] When the firm locates factory 1 at point M_1, the profits are derived as 3307. The firm can obtain the almost same profits when factory 1 is located within the area where the chaotic phenomenon appears.

[4]The phenomenon shown in Fig. 5.2 is a *chaos* or a *chaotic* phenomenon, which is generated from the Cauchy Convergence in the solution derivation process. The study to identify this phenomenon is not conducted in this section because this problem does not interfere with logical development. This issue will be discussed elsewhere.

[5]See the analysis by Ishikawa (2015b). The difference of the two profits may be estimated as less than 1 percent of the obtained profit.

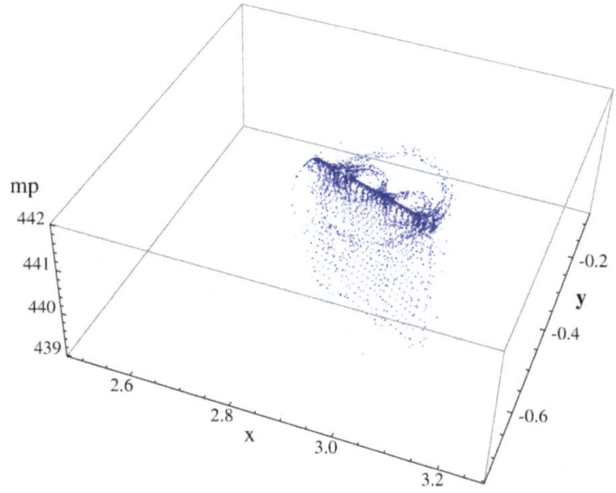

Fig. 5.2 Appearance of a chaotic phenomenon

5.3.2 Formation of the Location Prospective Area

As Fig. 5.2 shows, the optimal price can be fixed at 442, while the accurate optimal location site of factory 1 cannot be settled. The firm can, however, set up a kind of *location prospective area* (*LPA*) by referring to the chaotic phenomenon because the chaotic phenomenon is generated around the optimal point. As explained previously, if the manufacturer locates factory 1 within the range of the chaotic phenomenon, the profit of the firm is not far reduced from the optimal level. Thus, the firm could achieve a kind of the targeted profit. The area where a chaotic phenomenon appears is considered as a LPA for factory 1.

In addition, it could be said that even if the optimal location is identified, the firm may be unable to build factory 1 at the site for various reasons, such as weak ground, high land price, protracted bargaining, surrounding production circumstances, or living environments in real life. In this case, the firm needs to explore the next-best locational sites around the area in which the optimal site exists, setting up an LPA. The first step of the firm's location determination process, therefore, is to set up a LPA.

5.4 Firm's Profits and Revenues in Countries with Different Corporate Tax Rates

In the situation shown in Fig. 5.2, the firm's profit and revenues of the two countries are indicated in the first column of Table 5.1. Each column of Table 5.1 shows the transfer price, size of the LPA, price of the final goods, firm's profit and country's tax revenue.

Table 5.1 Variation of transfer price and firm's profits due to change of tax rates

Tax rates	$t = t^* = 0.82$	$t = t^* = 0.27$	$t = 0.70$, $t^* = 0.82$
Transfer price	442	442	417
Position of LPA	Small area near M_1	Large area near M_1	Small area near M_1
Price of final goods	551	551	545
Sale amount	49	49	55
Firm's profits	3307	13,417	5869
Y_1	2968	12,040	5293
Y_2	339	1377	576
Tax revenue, home	13,525	4453	12,350
Tax revenue, foreign	1544	509	2624

When the corporation tax rates of the two countries are reduced from 0.82 to 0.27, the LPA and the transfer price can be derived in the same way. The second column of Table 5.1 indicates the transfer price, LPA, price of the final goods, firm's profits, and country's tax revenue in this case.

When the corporation tax rates of the two countries are the same, the reduction of tax rates does not change the transfer price. The reduction of the tax rates increases of the size of the LPA. This fact implies that a wide LPA gives the firm many options in the determination of the factory's location.

The third column of Table 5.1 shows the results of the calculation when the combination of the tax rates is (t = 0.7, t^* = 0.82). It is interesting to see from Table 5.1 that the reduction of the corporate tax rate of the home country raises the transfer price and increases the tax revenues of the foreign country.

5.5 Location Power of the Corporate Tax and the Interest Rate

5.5.1 Assumptions for the Examination of Location Power of Corporate Tax Rates

Limiting the scope of the analysis to the firm's location problem, let us analyze the effects of the corporate tax rate on the factory's location and the transfer price. This analysis is conducted with the following assumptions: the freight rate of the lubricating oil, t_e, is increased from 0.01 to 0.5725. The corporate tax rate of the foreign country is fixed at 0.82, while the rate of the home country is reduced from 0.8 to 0.65, and then 0.6. The factory's location and the transfer price are derived for the three different tax rate combinations: (t = 0.8, t^* = 0.82), (t = 0.65 t^* = 0.82) and (t = 0.6, t^* = 0.82). The obtained result shows how the corporate tax rate exercises its power on the factory's location.

Fig. 5.3 LPA near the material M_1 when the corporate tax rate is relatively high

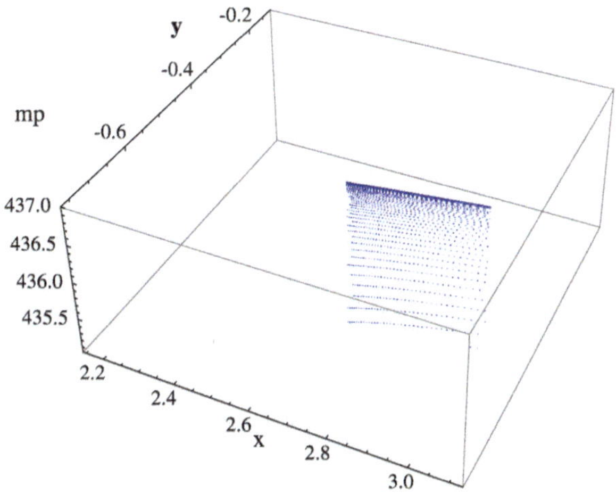

Table 5.2 LPA, transfer price, and profits for the three combination of tax rates

Tax rates	$t = 0.8$, $t^* = 0.82$	$t = 0.65$, $t^* = 0.82$	$t = 0.6$, $t^* = 0.82$
Position of LPA	Near point M_1	Near M_1 to point (0.4, −1.1)	Around point (0.4, −0.9)
Transfer price	437	411.5–412.4	407
Firm's profits	3681	6726–6788	7783

5.5.2 *Location of the Factory When the Corporate Tax Rate Is Relatively High*

Figure 5.3 shows the LPA when the corporation tax rate of the home country is relatively low, with the corporate tax rates combined ($t = 0.8$, $t^* = 0.82$). The LPA is formed near point M_1, and the transfer price is determined at 437. As the LPA is an almost a linear shape near point M_3, the firm locates factory 1 at a place on this linear area; it can obtain almost the same targeted profits, which can be estimated as 3681. The transfer price and the firm's profits are indicated in the first column of Table 5.2.

5.5.3 *Change of Position of LPA Due to a Reduction of the Corporate Tax Rate*

When the corporate tax rate of the home country decreases from 0.8 to 0.65, the corporate tax rate combination ($t = 0.65$, $t^* = 0.82$), a large LPA is formed from point M_1 to point (0.4, −1.1). Figure 5.4 depicts the large LPA. As shown in the

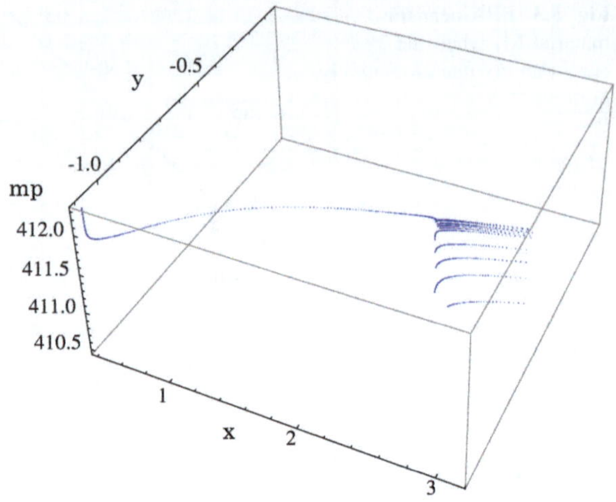

Fig. 5.4 Expansion of the LPA due to a reduction of the corporate tax rate

second column of Table 5.2, if the manufacturer locates factory 1 at point M_1 and sets the transfer price at 411.5, the firm obtains a profit of 6726. If the firm set factory 1 at (0.4, −1.1), the firm's profit is 6788. The difference between the firm's profits is 62, which is 0.92 percent against the firm's profit of 6726; therefore, the profit difference is very small even if the distance between the two potential location sites is far. This implies that if the manufacturer locates factory 1 within the LPA, the firm can obtain almost the same profits. It can be said that the firm obtains the targeted profits at every point within the LPA. A wider LPA provides the firm with more options in the determination of the factory's location.

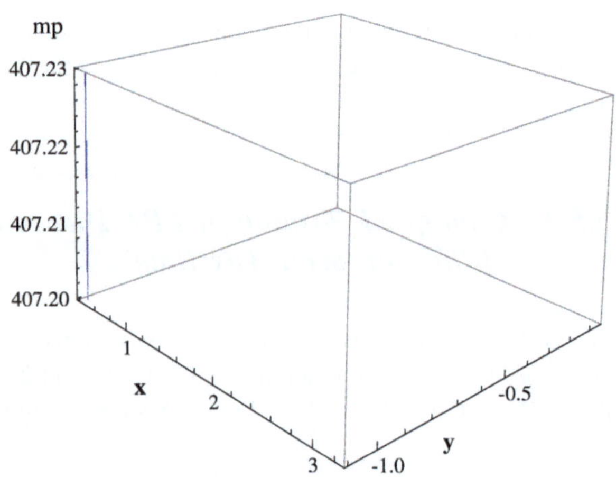

Fig. 5.5 Shift of the LPA when the corporate tax rate becomes relatively low

5.5.4 *Position of the LPA When the Corporate Tax Rate Is Relatively Low*

When the corporate tax rate of the home country becomes relatively low (0.6), the corporate tax rate combination is (t = 0.6, t^* = 0.82). The LPA is formed around point (0.4, −1.1). The transfer price of the intermediate goods is determined at 407. Figure 5.5 depicts the results of the calculation. The firm's profit is 7783, as shown in the third column of Table 5.2. It can be said that the reduction of the corporate tax rate in the home country alters the location pattern of factory 1 and 2.

Incorporating the results derived in the case when the freight rate of the lubricating oil t_e is 0.01 into consideration, the location power of corporate tax rate is explained as follows:

1. The reduction of the corporate tax rate of one country expands the LPA at the same position when the transportation cost is adequately low. The expansion of the LPA gives the firm more options in the determination of factory's location.
2. The reduction of the corporate tax rate shifts the position of the LPA from one place to another when the transportation cost is in a certain level. According to the change of position of the LPA, the firm shifts the location of the factory. It can be said that the corporate tax rate has strong location power to move the factory's location when the transportation cost is at a certain level.

5.5.5 *Location Power of the Interest Rate of the Country*

5.5.5.1 Firm's Profit Function as the Interest Rate Is Considered

A firm's activity is organized across borders. A manufacturer recognizes the interest rates in different countries as one of the important location factors. These interest rates affect the firm's profits, the firm's country selections, and location choices within the selected country.

In this section, the interest rates of countries are incorporated into the framework of the analysis used in the previous section. The interest rates of the home country and the foreign country are denoted by r and r^*, respectively. The term of the firm's production activity in question is represented by T.

If the firm achieves the profit indicated by Eq. (5.15) at every unit of time, the firm's total profit in the term of T, TY, is given by Eq. (5.18)[6]:

[6]By considering other factors that are closely related to the interest rate, such as the construction costs of a factory, the analysis can provide more comprehensive insights. Because the primary aim of this section is to just show that the interest rate has the location power, the analysis is conducted in the simplest framework.

$$TY = \int_0^T Y_1 e^{rt} dt + \int_0^T Y_2 e^{r*t} dt \tag{5.18}$$

Equation (5.18) is developed as Eq. (5.19).

$$\begin{aligned}TY = &((-1/r + (1/r)\text{Exp}(rT))(1-t)\Big[\Big(0.22\big(-206 + (582{,}409 - 900mp)^{0.5}\big)\Big)\Big((mp - t_g d_4) - (p_3 + t_e d_3)\Big)\\ &-2\Big(0.22\big(-206 + (582{,}409 - 900mp)^{0.5}\big)\Big)^{1.25} A^{-1.25}(p_1 + t_m d_1)^{0.5}(p_2 + t_m d_2)^{0.5} - F_1\Big]\\ &+(-1/r^* + (1/r^*)\text{Exp}(r * T))(1-t^*)\Big[\Big(600 - \Big(0.22\big(-206 + (582{,}409 - 900mp)^{0.5}\big)\Big)\\ &-mp\Big)\Big(0.22\big(-206 + (582{,}409 - 900mp)^{0.5}\big)\Big) - F_2\Big].\end{aligned} \tag{5.19}$$

From the profit function, the firm determines the optimal location of factory 1 and the transfer price of the intermediate goods in the same way as used in the previous section.

5.5.5.2 Shift of a Factory's Location Due to a Change of the Interest Rate

Let us derive the optimal location of factory 1 and the transfer price of the intermediate goods under the following assumptions. The transportation costs of the intermediate goods, t_g, and the lubricating oil, t_e, are assumed to be 0.675 and 0.01, respectively. The corporate tax rates of the home and the foreign country are fixed at 0.7 and 0.82, respectively. The term of the firm's production activity in question is 1.55. The interest rate of the foreign country is fixed at 0.1; that of the home

Fig. 5.6 Formation of an LPA near point M_1

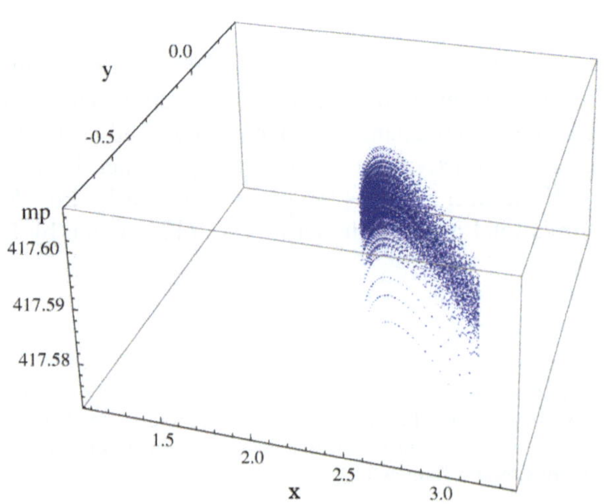

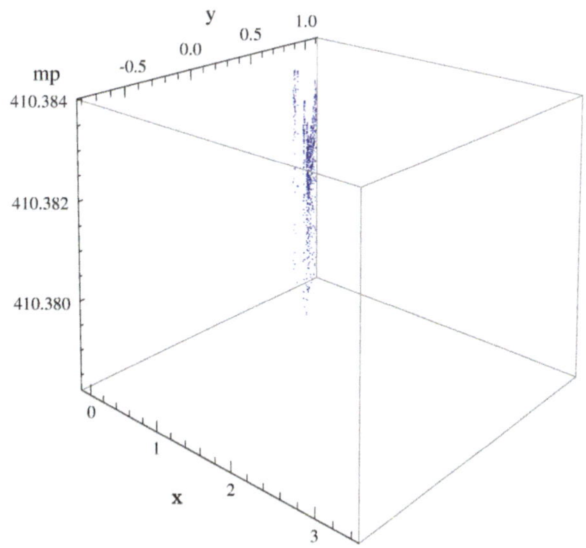

Fig. 5.7 Shift of the LPA due to a change of the interest rate

country is assumed initially to be 0.11, later being increased to 0.35. The values of the other parameters are the same as those assumed in the previous analysis.

When the interest rate of the home country is 0.11, the calculation results are shown in Fig. 5.6. From the chaotic phenomenon in Fig. 5.6, the LPA is set up near point M_1 and the transfer price is determined at 417.6. In this case, the firm locates factory 1 at a site within this LPA.

Then, we can derive the LPA and the transfer price when the interest rate of the home country is raised to 0.35. In the same way, the LPA and the transfer price are derived, as depicted in Fig. 5.7. The LPA is formed near the marketplace M_4 and the transfer price is set at 410.4. In this case, the firm locates factory 1 at a site within the LPA near market place M_4.

The comparison of Figs. 5.6 and 5.7 indicates that when the interest rate of the home country is changed from 0.11 to 0.35, the location of factory 1 shifts from a point near M_1 to a site near M_4. The change of the interest rate works to shift the location of the factory and change the transfer price. It can be said that the interest rate clearly exercises the locational power.

Because the interest rate of the foreign country is lower than that of the home country, factory 1 is not located at the marketplace where factory 2 exists. They just co-exist across the border between the countries. Although this location pattern seems to be an agglomeration, they do not make an agglomeration at the marketplace in the foreign country.[7]

[7]The location pattern in which manufacturing factories co-exist across borders can be identified at the border between Marisa and Singapore. For example, some Japanese manufacturing firms locates their factories across borders. The intermediate goods are moved between them using the

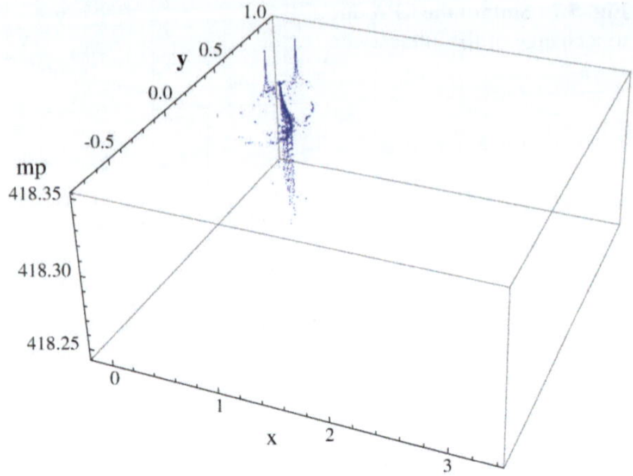

Fig. 5.8 Shift of an LPA by expansion of the activity term

5.5.5.3 Shift of Factory's Location by Expansion of the Term of Production Activity

Supposing that the term of the production activity of the firm is expanded from 1.55 to 1.75, let us analyze the effects of the term expansion on the factor's location. To this end, the interest rate of the home country is assumed back to 0.11. By applying the same method used in the previous sections, the results depicted in Fig. 5.8 are obtained.

Comparing Fig. 5.6 with Fig. 5.8, it is known that by the expansion of the term of the production activity, the position of the LPA is shifted from a point near M_1 to a site near the marketplace M_4; the transfer price is slightly raised from 417.6 to 418.4. That is, when the term of the planned production activity is relatively short, the firm locates factory 1 at a point near M_1. When the term is relatively long, factory 1 is located at a place near market M_4. It can be said that the location of factory 1 is influenced by the term of the firm's planned production activity.

(Footnote 7 continued)

tariff price, which is related to the transfer price in a sense, but its concept is different from the transfer price.

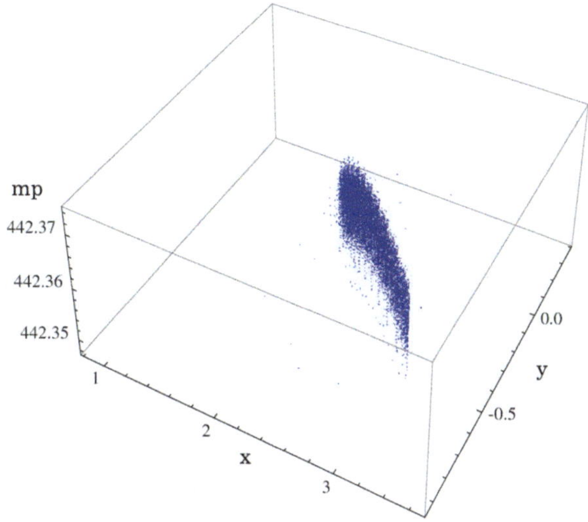

Fig. 5.9 Factory's location and transfer price with low production efficiency ($A = 1$)

5.6 Effects on a Factory's Location in an Industrial Park and Industrial Complex

5.6.1 Locational Shift of a Factory Due to an Increasing Change of Production Efficiency

In this section, incorporating new economic factors, economies of scope and scale economies, into the previous framework, the effects of a factory's location of an industrial park and industrial complex are analyzed. First, this section deals with the locational effects of an industrial park.

To examine the locational effects of an industrial park, the influences of the factory's production efficiency on its location is analyzed. The freight rate of the intermediate goods, t_g, is assumed to be 0.55, the corporation tax rates are changed to $t = t^* = 0.27$, and the interest rates are omitted for simplicity of the analysis.

Let us analyze the location power of the production efficiency of factory 1 by changing the value of parameter A from 1 to 2. When the efficiency of the factory is 1, $A = 1$, the location of factory 1 is derived in the same way as in the previous section.[8] The optimal location of factory 1 and the transfer price are determined within the LPA illustrated in Fig. 5.9.

When the production efficiency is low, $A = 1$, the transfer price of the intermediate goods is determined at 442 and factory 1 is located at a point near point M_1.

[8]Parameter A is often referred to as the *total factor productivity*. Romer (1990) analyzed the production efficiency by using the concept of ideas, and the results of the analysis are applied in many fields of economics.

Table 5.3 Firm's production amount, profits, and tax revenues ($A = 1$)

Factory's location	Production amount	Profits	Tax revenue, *H*	Tax revenue, *F*
Around M_1	49	13,350	4434	504

H home country, *F* foreign country

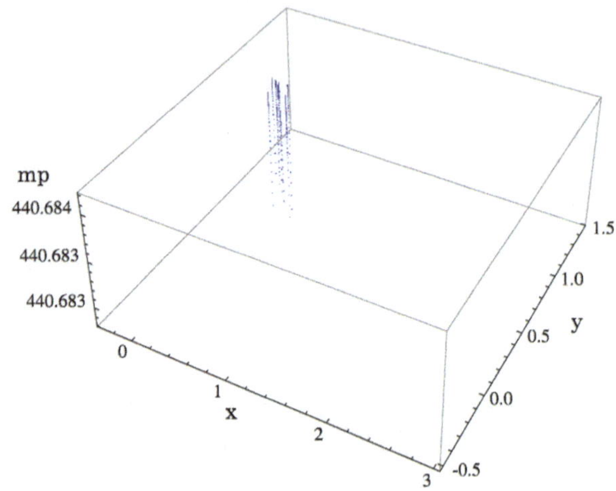

Fig. 5.10 Factory's location and transfer price with higher production efficiency ($A = 2$)

Table 5.4 Firm's production amount, profits, and tax revenues ($A = 2$)

Factory's location	Production amount	Profits	Tax revenue, *H*	Tax revenue, *F*
Around M_4	50	13,589	4503	527

H home country, *F* foreign country

In this case, the firm's production amount, profits, and tax revenues of the two countries are indicated by Table 5.3.

Then, if the production efficiency of factory 1 is increased from 1 to 2, $A = 2$, the transfer price and the factory's location are changed. They are indicated by Fig. 5.10. The transfer price is slightly reduced to 440.7 and the factory's location is shifted to a point near marketplace M_4. The firm's production amount, profits, and tax revenues of the two countries in this case are indicated by Table 5.4.

The results shown in Tables 5.3 and 5.4 imply that an increase of the production efficiency of factory 1 moves the factory's location toward the marketplace and increases the production amount, firm's profits, and tax revenues of the two countries.

The transfer price and the location of the factory are not analyzed here when the freight rates of the intermediate goods are much lower than 0.55 and much higher than 0.55. However, in both cases, the production efficiency loses its locational power. When the freight rate is low, $t_g = 0.225$, the LPA remains at a point near the material point M_1. When the freight rate is higher, $t_g = 0.625$, the LPA does not move from a point near the market point M_4. It can be concluded that the freight rates of the intermediate goods have stronger location power than the production efficiency in the cases when the freight rates are adequately high and low. As shown in the above analysis, however, when the freight rates are at a moderate level, the production efficiency of the factory has location power to shift the LPA. As the production efficiency of the factory increases, the factory shifts toward the marketplace at which the goods produced by the factory are used.

5.6.2 *Relationship Between the Location of the Industrial Park and Production Efficiency*

This section shifts the focus of the analysis to a location policy of the government that plans to build an industrial park to attract factory 1 into the home country.[9] Incorporating economies of scope and scale economies into the previous framework of the analysis, this subsection analyzes the location of an industrial park considering the freight rates of the firm's intermediate goods.[10]

5.6.2.1 Industrial Park that Aims to Improve Production Efficiency and Its Location

In this section, two new assumptions are set:

1. The government of the home country constructs an industrial park which aims to improve the production efficiency of factory 1 by confining the manufacturing types to one similar to factory 1.
2. If the firm's two production processes agglomerate at the marketplace in the foreign country, economies of scope work to reduce the fixed cost of factory 1 by 200. The reduction of the fixed cost of factory 1 works to attract factory 1 to the marketplace.

In addition, it is supposed in this section that the freight rates of the intermediate goods are assumed to be two different levels, 0.85 and 0.225; the corporate tax rates of the two countries are assumed to be the same, $t = t^* = 0.82$. Other parameters' values are the same those used in the previous sections.

---

[9]The industrial complex invites various kinds of manufacturing factories more than the industrial park. Thus, the former is larger than the latter.

[10]Needless to say, the government would not construct an industrial park only to attract a small fragmented production process from a foreign country to its territory. However, the analysis of an industrial park in this context provides locational policy-makers with a useful theoretical insight to analyze the relationships between the factory's location and the characteristics of an industrial park.

Table 5.5 The difference of profits by different location patterns with a high freight rate

Location pattern	Transfer price	Production amount	Firm's profits
Co-existing across border	443	48.97	3279
Agglomeration at M_4	443	48.97	3315

5.6.2.2 Location of an Industrial Park in a High Freight Rate of Intermediate Goods

When the freight rate of the intermediate goods is high, $t_g = 0.85$, and if economies of scope by consolidating the two production processes at the market place would *not* work, factory 1 would be located at a point near the marketplace M_4 within the home country. In this case, by using the same calculation method, the transfer price and the production amount are derived as 443 and 48.97, and the firm's profit is 3279.

Keeping the transfer price as 443 and production amount as 48.97, when the firm can reduce the fixed cost of factory 1 by 200 with consolidating the two factories in the marketplace, the firm's profit increases from 3279 to 3315. The transfer price, production amount, and firm's profit in these cases are shown in Table 5.5. The firm decides to consolidate the two factories in the marketplace in the foreign country in order to obtain the higher profits of 3315.

Now, if the consolidation of the two factories is realized in the marketplace of the foreign country, the corporate tax revenue of the home country becomes zero. It is thus considered that the government of the home country plans to build an industrial park, which is oriented to improve the production efficiency of factory 1, in order to attract factory 1 to its territory. The location of the industrial park is easily determined from the previous analysis in which the freight rate is assumed to be $t_g = 0.85$; the location is determined at a point near marketplace M_4 within the home country

Now, let us analyze how much the industrial park must improve the production efficiency of factory 1 in order for factory 1 to depart from the marketplace to the territory of the home country. The necessary production efficiency of factory 1 that the industrial park needs to achieve is obtained by solving Eq. (5.20) with respect to A:

Table 5.6 Tax revenues when the industrial park improves the production efficiency ($t_g = 0.85$)

Production efficiency	Location pattern	Tax revenue, *H*	Tax revenue, *F*
2.34	Co-existing across border	13,595	1506

$$
\begin{aligned}
&(1-0.82)*\left((600-Q)*Q-443*Q-1.5*Q*(2+Q)^2/200-2500\right)\\
&\quad+(1-0.82)*\left(Q*\left(443-0.85*(0+0)^{0.5'}-\left(0.2+0.01*\left(0+(1+1.5)^2\right)^{0.5}\right)\right)\right.\\
&\quad-2*A^{-1.25}*Q^{1.25}*\left(0.25+0.11\left((0+3)^2+(1+0.5)^2\right)^{0.5}\right)^{0.5}\\
&\qquad\left.*\left(2+0.11'\left((0+3^{0.5})^2+(1+0.5)^2\right)^{0.5'}\right)^{0.5}-5000\right)-3315=0
\end{aligned}
\tag{5.20}
$$

where Q is 48.97. From Eq. (5.20), the necessary level of the production efficiency is derived as 2.34, $A = 2.34$. It is concluded that if the industrial park is constructed at a point near the marketplace and it provides factory 1 with a production efficiency of more than 2.34, the government of the home country can move factory 1 from the marketplace in the foreign country to the home country. When the government of the home country succeeds in attracting the factory to its territory, the location pattern of the factories and the tax revenues are as shown in Table 5.6.

5.6.2.3 Location of an Industrial Park in Low Freight Rate of Intermediate Goods

When the freight rate of the intermediate goods is low, $t_g = 0.225$, and if economies of scope in the marketplace would *not* work by consolidating the two production processes in the marketplace, factory 1 would be located at a point near the material point M_1. The transfer price is 442, the production amount is 49.19, and the firm's profit is 3307.

Keeping the transfer price at 442 and production amount at 49.19, when the location of factory 1 is shifted to make a consolidation of two factories in the marketplace, the fixed cost of factory 1 is reduced by 200. In this case, the firm's profits increase to 3332. In the two cases, the transfer price, production amount, and firm's profits are shown in Table 5.7. Consequently, the firm locates factory 1 at the marketplace in the foreign country to obtain the higher profits of 3332.

Table 5.7 Difference of profits by different location patterns with low freight rate ($t_g = 0.225$)

Location pattern	Transfer price	Production amount	Firm's profits
M_1–M_4	442	49.19	3307
Agglomeration at M_4	442	49.19	3332

Then, the government of the home country would determine a plan to construct an industrial park to attract factory 1 to its territory. In this case, considering the results of the preceding analysis in which the freight rates are assumed to be 0.225, the location of the industrial park is determined near the material point M_1. The necessary production efficiency of factory 1 that the industrial park needs to achieve is obtained by solving Eq. (5.21) with respect to A:

$$\begin{aligned}
&(1-0.82)*\left((600-Q)*Q-442*Q-1.5*Q*(2+Q)^2/200-2500\right)\\
&\quad+(1-0.82)*\left(Q*\left(442-0.225*\left(3^2+1.5^2\right)^{0.5\prime}-\left(0.2+0.01*\left(3^2+1^2\right)^{0.5}\right)\right)\right.\\
&\quad-2*A^{-1.25}*Q^{1.25}*\left(0.25+0.11\left(0^2+0^2\right)^{0.5}\right)^{0.5}\\
&\quad*\left(2+0.11\left(\left(3+3^{0.5}\right)^2+0^2\right)^{0.5\prime}\right)^{0.5}-5000)-3332=0
\end{aligned} \tag{5.21}$$

where Q is 49.19. From Eq. (5.21), the level of production efficiency of factory 1 that the park must achieve is derived as 2.38, A = 2.38.

However, based on the fact shown in Sect. 5.2 that factory 1 with high production efficiency is located at a point near the marketplace, the government plans to establish an industrial park near the marketplace. In this case, the level of production efficiency that the industrial park needs to attain is derived as 2.32 by solving Eq. (5.21a) with respect to A:

$$\begin{aligned}
&(1-0.82)*\left((600-Q)*Q-442*Q-1.5*Q*(2+Q)^2/200-2500\right)\\
&\quad+(1-0.82)*\left(Q*\left(442-0.225*(0+0)^{0.5\prime}-\left(0.2+0.01*\left(0+(1+1.5)^2\right)^{0.5}\right)\right)\right.\\
&\quad-2*A^{-1.25}*Q^{1.25}*\left(0.25+0.11\left((0+3)^2+(1+0.5)^2\right)^{0.5}\right)^{0.5}\\
&\quad*\left(2+0.11^{\prime}\left(\left(0+3^{0.5}\right)^2+(1+0.5)^2\right)^{0.5\prime}\right)^{0.5}-5000\Big)-3332=0
\end{aligned} \tag{5.21a}$$

If the government of the home country establishes an industrial park near the marketplace, the government can attract factory 1 to its territory by constructing an industrial park that achieves a production efficiency of 2.32, less than 2.38. Therefore, the government constructs the industrial park at point near the marketplace within its territory. Table 5.8 shows the location pattern of the factories and tax revenues of the two countries when the park provides a production efficiency of 2.32.

It is concluded based on this analysis that if the industrial park aims to increase the production efficiency of factory 1, then the location of the industrial park is determined to be at a point near marketplace M_4 regardless of the freight rates of

Table 5.8 Tax revenues when the industrial park improves the production efficiency at point M_4

Production efficiency	Location pattern	Tax revenue, *H*	Tax revenue, *F*
2.32	Co-existing across border	13634	1543

intermediate goods.[11] Moreover, it is noteworthy that even if the freight rates of the intermediate goods become considerably low, the level of the production efficiency that the industrial park needs to achieve to attract factory 1 to the home country does not change much.

5.6.3 *Industrial Complex Aiming to Reduce Fixed Costs and Its Location*

It is supposed in this section that the government plans to construct an industrial complex to attract factory 1 to its territory from the marketplace; in addition, the industrial complex aims to reduce the fixed cost of factory 1 by scale economies that are generated by inducing various types of manufacturing factories to the industrial complex. For this situation, this section examines the location of an industrial complex and the necessary level of scale economies the industrial complex needs to attain.

5.6.3.1 Location of the Industrial Complex with a High Freight Rate of Intermediate Goods

When the freight rate of intermediate goods is at a high level, $t_g = 0.85$, the firm's situation is described by Table 5.5. That is, because the economies of scope by consolidating the two production processes in the marketplace work to reduce the fixed cost of factory 1 by 200, the firm locates factory 1 in the marketplace in the foreign country. Thus, the government of the home country plans to establish an industrial complex that reduces the fixed cost of factory 1 by scale economies to attract the factory to its territory. Let us analyze the location of the industrial complex and the necessary reduction of the fixed costs to attract factory 1 from the marketplace to the home country.

If the freight rate of the intermediate goods is high, $t_g = 0.85$, factory 1 would be located near the marketplace of the foreign country. The reduction of the fixed cost of factory 1, which the industrial complex needs to attract the factory to the home country, is derived by solving Eq. (5.22) with respect to *E*:

[11] As long as the corporate tax rates of the two countries are the same, the level of the tax rates does not influence the production efficiency that is needed to attract the factory to the home country.

$$(1-0.82)*\left((600-Q)*Q-442*Q-1.5*Q*(2+Q)^2/200-2500\right)$$
$$+(1-0.82)*\left(Q*\left(442-0.85*(0+0)^{0.5'}-\left(0.2+0.01*\left(0+(1+1.5)^2\right)^{0.5}\right)\right)\right.$$
$$-2*1^{-1.25}*Q^{1.25}*\left(0.25+0.11\left((0+3)^2+(1+0.5)^2\right)^{0.5}\right)^{0.5}$$
$$\left.*\left(2+0.11'\left(\left(0+3^{0.5}\right)^2+(1+0.5)^2\right)^{0.5'}\right)^{0.5}-(5000-E)\right)-3315=0 \tag{5.22}$$

where the production efficiency of factory 1 is 1, $A = 1$; the value of 3315 in Eq. (5.22) indicates the firm's profit in the case that consolidation of the two factories would be realized at the marketplace. From Eq. (5.22), the necessary reduction of the fixed cost of factory 1 is obtained as 200, which is the same that the firm would enjoy by consolidating the two factories in the marketplace.

5.6.3.2 Location of the Industrial Complex with a Low Freight Rate of Intermediate Goods

When the freight rate of intermediate goods is at a low level, $t_g = 0.225$, the situation of the firm is described by Table 5.7. Let us analyze the location of the industrial complex and the necessary reduction of the fixed cost of factory 1 to attract the factory to the home country when the freight rate is low.

When the freight rate of the intermediate goods is low, $t_g = 0.225$, and there are no economies of scope in the market, factory 1 is located near material point M_1. However, when the firm can reduce the fixed cost of factory 1 by 200 by consolidating the two factories in the marketplace, the firm locates factory 1 at the marketplace in the foreign country. Thus, the government plans to build an industrial complex in order to attract factory 1 to the home country. In this case, the government constructs the industrial complex near the material point M_1. The reduction of the fixed cost of factory 1 that the industrial complex needs to attain is derived by solving Eq. (5.23) with respect to E:

Table 5.9 The freight rate and the industrial complex's location and necessary reduction

Freight rate	Location of industrial complex	Necessary reduction of fixed cost
0.85	Near market M_4	200
0.225	Near point M_1	137

$$
\begin{aligned}
&(1-0.82)*\left((600-Q)*Q-442*Q-1.5*Q*(2+Q)^2/200-2500\right)\\
&\quad+(1-0.82)*\left(Q*\left(442-0.225*(3^2+1.5^2)^{0.5'}-\left(0.2+0.01*(3^2+1^2)^{0.5}\right)\right)\right.\\
&\quad-2*1^{-1.25}*Q^{1.25}*\left(0.25+0.11\,(0^2+0^2)^{0.5}\right)^{0.5}\\
&\quad\left.*\left(2+0.11\left((3+3^{0.5})^2+0^2\right)^{0.5'}\right)^{0.5}-(5000-E)\right)-3332=0
\end{aligned}
\tag{5.23}
$$

where the value of 3332 in Eq. (5.23) is the firm's profit when the consolidation is realized at the market place. From Eq. (5.23), the necessary reduction of the fixed cost of factory 1 to attract factory 1 to the home country is obtained as 137, which is less than the value of 200 that the firm could enjoy in the marketplace. Table 5.9 shows the relationships between the freight rates of the intermediate goods, location of the industrial complex, and the necessary reduction of the fixed cost that the industrial complex needs to achieve. As shown by Table 5.9, as the freight rate decreases, the location of the industrial complex changes to a point near M_1 from a point near M_4, and the necessary reduction of the fixed cost is greatly reduced.

5.6.4 *Effects of Improving the Industrial Park and Industrial Complex on the Manufacturing Firm*

As shown in the above analysis, when the freight rate of the intermediate goods is 0.225, the industrial park is planned to improve *the production efficiency*, the corporate tax rates of the countries are the same at $t = t^* = 0.82$, the industrial park is located near the marketplace M_4, the park provides factory 1 with a production

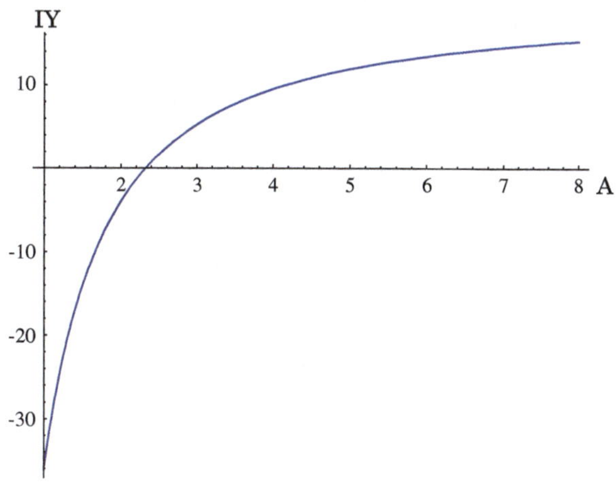

Fig. 5.11 Increment of a firm's profits by increasing the production efficiency

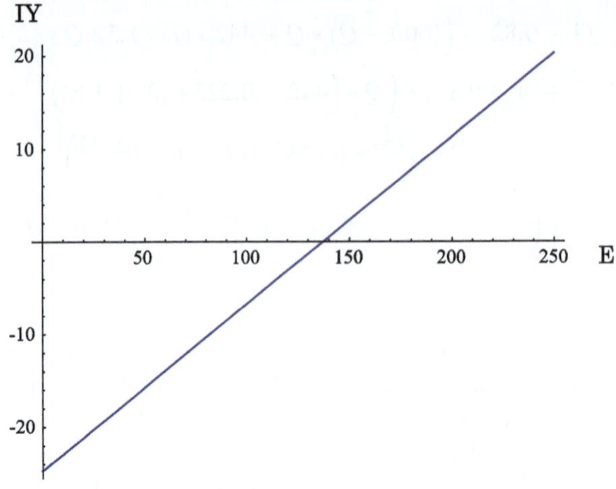

Fig. 5.12 Increment of a firm's profits by increasing the reduction of the fixed cost

efficiency of more than 2.32, and the firm obtains a profit of 3332 at the industrial park.

Based on this situation, this section first examines how the firm's profit increases from the level of the profit of 3332 by increasing the production efficiency of factory 1 at the industrial park. Figure 5.11 illustrates the relationship between the increase of the production efficiency of factory 1 and the increment of the firm's profit, *IY*, from the profit level of 3332. As indicated by Fig. 5.11, when the production efficiency of factory 1 is 2.32, the firm's profit is 3332; thus, the increment of the profits is just zero. As the production efficiency increases from 2.32, the firm's profit becomes higher, but the increment of the profit is slight. Thus, even if the industrial park offers the factory a considerably higher production efficiency, the increment of the firm's profit is small. This industrial park will not be enlarged because the enlargement does not contribute much to the increase of the firm's profit.

Then, based on the same situation, suppose that the government of the home country builds an industrial complex near the material point M_1, which contains various types of manufacturing firms, and it aims to reduce the fixed cost of factory 1. Figure 5.12 describes the relationship between the reduction of the fixed cost, *E*, and the increment of the firm's profit. When the reduction of the fixed cost of factory 1 is 137, the firm's profit is 3332 and the increment of the firm's profit is just zero. As the reduction of the fixed cost increases from 137, the firm's profit increases at the same rate; the increment of the firm's profit is the constant. Thus, this industrial complex will be enlarged to provide the manufacturing firm with scale economies, and it contributes to increasing the firm's profit. It is thus considered that the industrial complex is likely to be enlarged by inviting various sorts of manufacturing firms and factories.

5.6.5 Differences Between an Industrial Park and Industrial Complex in Location Policy Making

It is considered from the above analyses that if an industrial park is oriented to improve the production efficiency of factories, the types of manufacturing factories in the park are confined to a narrow range. The industrial park is planned to provide a specific and small-scale infrastructure to similar kinds of factories; the construction costs to establish the industrial park tend to be relatively low. When an industrial complex aims to reduce the fixed costs of many factories, the industrial complex tends to be large to induce various kinds of manufacturing factories to the complex: Because the fixed costs of the factories consist of various costs that are related to the production facility and logistics, the industrial complex must invite various kinds of factories that collectively use the large infrastructure to efficiently operate the industrial complex. The construction costs of the complex tend to be relatively high.

The government of the home country may not spend much money to develop industrial activity in a region. It may be considered in the home country that the government establishes an industrial park that aims to improve the production efficiency. The industrial park may be located within its territory near the marketplace in the foreign country. The industrial park may help to develop industrial society by introducing factories from an existing industrial country with relatively low costs. If the freight rates of intermediate goods are adequately low and the government of the home country can afford to construct an industrial complex, an industrial complex that aims to reduce the fixed costs of factories is established. The location of the industrial complex is not confined to being near a marketplace. In addition, the industrial complex induces many sorts of manufacturing factories to the country and may help to increase industrial composition in the country.

Lastly, as clarified in preceding section, the level of a firm's profit within a locational prospective area is maintained at almost the same level. That is, the factory of the firm is not limited to a specific site, but the factory's location is so-called footloose within the LPA. This fact can be applied to the location determination of the industrial park and the industrial complex: Factories can move into an industrial park and an industrial complex if they are within a firm's LPAs. The governments of the countries, therefore, will be able to construct an industrial park and industrial complex within a certain spatial range by considering various regional economic conditions according to the principle of the satisfaction maximization.

Part III
Location Theory of City System

Chapter 6
City Systems Built on the Basis of Economic Activity

Economic globalization gives rise to a harsher cost competition among manufacturing firms. It follows that manufacturing firms' production processes are fragmented into small blocs, which are scattered over a large geographical space. The locations of factories that use the fragmented production processes are usually near cities because workers' daily lives are sustained by the many kinds of retailers and social facilities available in cities. Workers' lives are not only sustained by cities but also city systems within a region. The structure of a city system affects the production efficiency of firms through the quality of laborers' daily lives. The city system has become important to manufacturing firms, which select a region in a large geographical area for the location of their factories.

The contents of a city system may reveal the general performance of a regional economy. At the same time, a city system within a region may be one of factors that determines the progress direction of the regional economy. Therefore, a city system and the networks of cities are significant factors in the revitalization of a regional economy.[1,2] The regional government can intervene and alter the progress direction of its region by changing the city system.

Part 3 of this book is organized as follows. First, a theoretical city system is analyzed by using the retailers' market areas and cities' production functions. Second, the analysis is expanded to include the relationship between the internal structures of the cities and the contents of the city system. The distribution of cities' economic volumes within a city system is examined in relation to the land rents of the cities' internal areas. Third, the relationships between the city systems and the social and economic performances achieved in regions are examined using Japanese data.

[1]The significance of the city system was clearly pointed out by Capello (2004, 2007).
[2]See the work of Sassen (1991) on cities' features in the global economy.

T. Ishikawa, *Dynamic Locational Phases of Economic Activity in the Globalized World*, DOI 10.1007/978-981-10-0524-4_6

6.1 City Systems Constructed on the Basis of Market Area Theory

6.1.1 City Systems by Traditional Market Area Theory

As is well known, there are two city system theories that are built on the basis of the retailers' market areas: the theories by Christaller (1933) and Lösch (1940). They constructed the central place system (city system, hereafter) by using different-sized market areas of different kinds of retailers. The places at which the retailers co-exist make up the primary economic core of cities. It is said, thus, that these two theories provide a foundation to explain theoretically the city systems.[3]

Although the theories both use the retailers' market areas to build a city system, there is a crucial difference between them from the viewpoint of microeconomics. The retailers' market areas used by Christaller in construction of a city system emerged under a pseudo-monopoly economic condition. The retailers usually enjoy positive profits before new retailers enter into the market space to jeopardize their market areas. After a series of new retailers enter into the places at which the existing retailers are located and the apexes of the existing retailers' market areas, many retailers can enjoy positive profits. To re-construct a city system according to Christaller's theory, therefore, is relatively easy.

On the other hand, reconstructing a city system according to Lösch's theory is very difficult. All kinds of retailers' market areas used by Lösch are generated under the Lösch competitive equilibrium. It is thus supposed in the Lösch theory that the market area size of every kind of retailer is the smallest market area in each kind of spatial competitive equilibrium. Because all existing retailers obtain no positive profit, if new retailers jeopardize the existing retailers' market areas, no retailer survives in the market space. In this situation, Lösch devised a way to construct a city system as follows. First, setting all networks of the market areas of all kinds of retailers on a plane space, these networks are different from each other in their mesh size. Second, all networks of the market areas are rotated in order for the retailers' locations to co-exist as often as possible. The places at which retailers co-exist have a robust economic core for the formation of a city, and the places are ranked according to the number of the retailers in the place. Consequently, various-sized cities are generated to build a city system in the plane space. This city system has diversity in cities' sizes and a strong microeconomic base. It is, however, difficult to understand the logic of building a city system and the construction method is too artificial to reconstruct the city system.

In addition to these two traditional city system theories, there is an interesting theory on building a city system by using the retailers' market areas in free-entry

---

[3]Parr (1978) and Ishikawa and Toda (2000) expanded the city system theory from the viewpoint of the microeconomic theory. Parr (1988) and Tinbergen (1968) analyzed the city system from macroeconomic viewpoints. The work of Zipf (1941) may contribute to the analysis of city systems.

competitive equilibria. This theory applies the contact price curve (CPC) to construct a city system.[4] This alternative approach is referred to here as the *flexible market area theory* (FMAT). This approach uses the CPC to select the market area sizes in constructing a city system. It is supposed in the FMAT that all retailers are under free-entry competitive equilibria; no retailers can obtain positive profit from their market areas. However, the sizes of the market areas available to construct a city system are not limited to the smallest market area size. That is, in the Lösch theory, the retailers' market area size is limited to the smallest market area size for each kind of retailer. In the FMAT, various-sized market areas become available to build a city system. Because the market area size is not limited to one size, FMAT has flexibility in building a city system by using various-sized market areas that are generated in free-entry competitive equilibria.

6.1.2 City System in a Spatial Competitive Market Space

Let us construct a city system by FMAT that utilizes the market areas indicated by the CPC. It is assumed in this section that all kinds of retailers are under spatial free-entry equilibria and their market area shape is confined to a hexagon.

Based on the analysis of the CPC developed in Chap. 3, a CPC is given by Eq. (6.1). Each parameter is assumed to be assigned the following numerical values: the retailer's marginal cost, $k = 0$; fixed cost, $F = 0.05a^4$; and transportation cost per mile, $t = 1$. The CPC is described by the curve of *L–GO–E* in Fig. 6.1.

$$\begin{aligned}\mathrm{CPC} = {} & 0.5(a + 1.6072tU + k \\ & - ((a - 2 \cdot 3^{0.5}0.2027tU - k)^2 - 2 \cdot 3^{0.5}F/3U^2)^{0.5})\end{aligned} \tag{6.1}$$

The CPC shows all radiuses of the inscribed circles of the market areas on the horizontal axis and all delivered prices at the apexes of the hexagonal market areas are indicated by the vertical axis. Point L on the CPC indicates the Lösch equilibrium, and point GO (which is on the lowest side of the curve) indicates the Greenhut-Ohta equilibrium. All market area sizes indicated by the CPC can be available to construct a city system at the first stage of competition among retailers. Using this fact, a city system that has some layers can be easily built without rotating the networks of retailers' market areas.

Figure 6.2 shows a city system that is constructed using the market areas indicated by the two CPCs. One of the curves is shown by Fig. 6.1. In the construction of the city system, four different kinds of retailers are assumed. The retailers are classified in descending order –L, M, S, and H– in Fig. 6.2. Large retailers (L) have the largest market areas, Middle-sized retailers (M) have the second largest market

[4]As mentioned in Chap. 3, CPC has almost the same essence of the frontier price curve, which was devised by Hoover (1970).

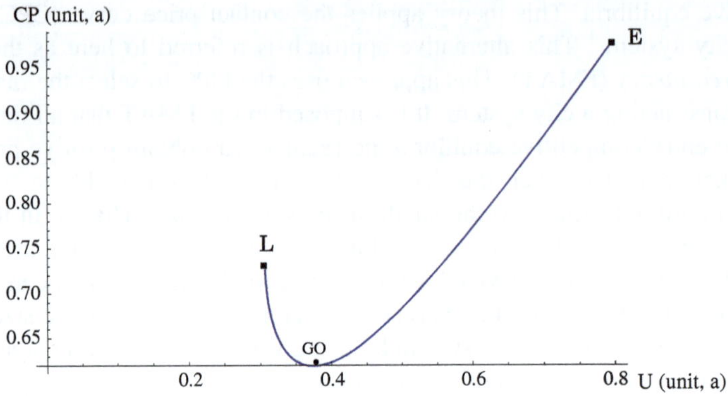

Fig. 6.1 Contact price curve

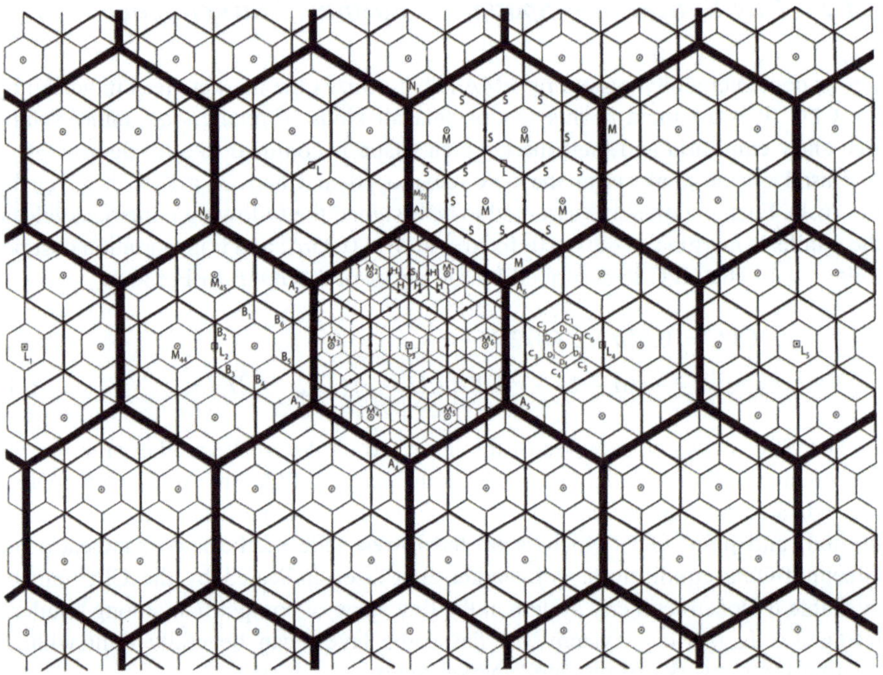

Fig. 6.2 A city system constructed by flexible market area theory

areas, and small retailers (H) have the small market areas. Referring to the CPC in Fig. 6.1, the radius of the inscribed circle of the largest market area of the L retailers is assumed to be 0.8a and that of the M retailers is 0.32a. The bold lines in Fig. 6.2 indicate the market areas of the largest retailers. Points L_i (i = 1, 3, 5) show the locations of the largest retailers. A retailer of each group is located at points L_i (i = 1, 3, 5). These L points become the largest cities. Although the largest retailers are located at points L_i (i = 2, 4), M retailers do not locate at these points L_i (i = 2, 4). These points L_i (i = 2, 4) become the relatively fragile large cities.

Subsequently, at point M, a retailer of each of the three groups M, S, and H co-exist. Point M becomes the medium cities. Similarly, at point S, a retailer of each of the S and H groups co-exist. Point S becomes small-sized cities. Lastly, at point H, only very small retailers H are located, which have a very small market area. These points become the towns.[5] The radius of the inscribed circle of the market area of the retailers S is $0.16a$ and that of the retailers H is $0.08a$. The radiuses of the inscribed circles of the market areas are derived from another CPC, in which the fixed cost is assumed to be smaller than $F = 0.05a^4$. FMAT can build a city system without the rotating the network of the market meshes on a free-entry competitive market space.

6.1.3 *Change of a City System Due to a Reduction of Transportation Costs*

City systems change as transportation technology progresses. This section analyzes how a reduction in transportation costs changes an existing city system. As shown in Chap. 2, the size of the retailers' market areas changes due to a reduction of transportation costs, and the direction of the change is different according to the competition style among retailers. As the transportation cost decreases, the market areas of the small retailers, such as convenience stores, become smaller. It is inferred that because this entry of retailers into the market space tends to be easier, small cities that are grounded on these small retailers do not have much risk of being expelled from the market space. The number of small cities, which are shown by points S and H in Fig. 6.2, remains at almost the same level or the number tends to increase as the transportation cost is reduced.

As the transportation cost decreases, the market areas of the large and middle retailers, which are classified into groups L and M in the above subsection, become larger. This subsection, selecting the middle-sized retailers, analyzes the change of the city system due to the expansion of the market areas of the middle retailers. As the transportation cost is reduced, some of the medium retailers are forced to be expelled from the market space by the competition among them. Some cities from which the medium retailers are expelled from the retailing industry reduce their retailing functions. As a result, these medium cities, which are at point M in Fig. 6.2, reduce their rank in terms of retailing volume and population, and they become classified to the group of the small cities. Figures 6.3 and 6.4 explain the change in the medium cities due to a reduction of the transportation cost.

Figure 6.3 shows the original network of the market areas of the middle-sized retailers on the basis of the city system shown in Fig. 6.2. In this market area

---

[5]Point C in Fig. 6.2 indicates villages or very small towns.

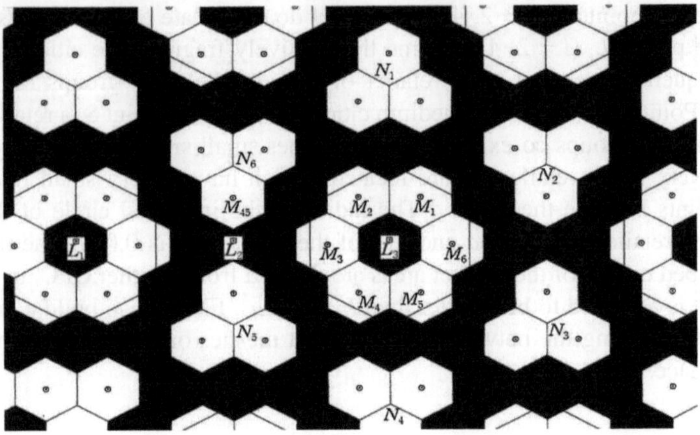

Fig. 6.3 Market structure of middle-sized retailers

Fig. 6.4 Market area shapes and network of the middle-sized retailers

situation, as mentioned in the previous section, the middle sized retailers at the largest points L_i ($i = 1, 3, 5$) have potentially advantageous sales conditions because they can easily expand their market areas as the transportation costs are reduced.

On the other hand, the retailers at points M_i ($i = 1, 2, 3, 4, 5, 6$) that do not have an advantage are forced to be expelled from the market space by losing parts of their market areas to a rival retailer that locates at point L_3. Consequently, the six cities at points M_i ($i = 1, 2, 3, 4, 5, 6$) reduce the retailing functions. By a similar reason, the retailer at point M_{45} and two retailers that are located in the northern side of point M_{45} in Fig. 6.2 disappear. The parts in white in Fig. 6.3 show the areas that are abandoned by the retailers being expelled from the market space.

These abandoned areas offer an opportunity for potential retailers to enter at points N_i ($i = 1, 2, 3, 4, 5, 6$) because each of these white areas is large enough for a new retailer to locate if the new retailer sets a higher retail price and has a smaller market area compared to existing retailers. The new retailer's location point N_i ($i = 1, 2, 3, 4, 5, 6$) provides an opportunity to be a city. Figure 6.4 shows the new network of the market areas of the middle-sized retailers, which resulted from the reduction of transportation costs. From Figs. 6.3 and 6.4, it could be said that due to the reduction of the transportation cost, the location pattern and the number of the second largest cities are dramatically varied; the number of these cities decreases and their market area size becomes larger; and the market area shape diversifies into the four shapes. The shape of the market area boundary between the retailers is different, with a straight line and hyperbola, because their prices at the stores of the retailers are different. Lastly, because the reduction of the transportation cost expels the retailers, the surviving retailers obtain positive profits. In addition, the retailers' profits are different from each other because the surviving retailers have different retail prices and the different market area sizes as described in Fig. 6.4.

It could be said that the retailers' location pattern, which was established in an early stage of economic development, is dramatically altered by a reduction of the transportation cost. The economic situation of a city system also varies with a reduction of the transportation cost.

6.2 City System Built by Using Cities' Production Functions

6.2.1 *Assumptions and Framework*

This section analyzes the structure of a city system from the supply side and introduces cities' production functions into the analysis instead of the using the retailers' market areas. The aim of this section is to show a mechanism of the change of the distribution patterns of city's population and its production amount within a city system. This section sets the following assumptions and the framework to proceed with the analysis.

There are four cities in a region, which have different production conditions. These cities are denoted as city A, B, C, D, respectively. They produce the same kind of goods by different production functions. Each city's production function is given by Eq. (6.2i), i = A, B, C, D:

$$Q_{\mathrm{A}} = 1.25P_{\mathrm{A}}^{2}\,\mathrm{EXP}(-0.16P_{\mathrm{A}}) \tag{6.2A}$$

$$Q_{\mathrm{B}} = 1.2P_{\mathrm{B}}^{1.85}\,\mathrm{EXP}(-0.25P_{\mathrm{B}}) \tag{6.2B}$$

$$Q_C = 1.1 P_C^{1.2}\,\mathrm{EXP}(-0.15 P_C) \tag{6.2C}$$

$$Q_D = 4 P_D^{2.5}\,\mathrm{EXP}(-0.8 P_D) \tag{6.2D}$$

where Q_i (i = A, B, C, D) is the production amount of each city. The production amount is a function of a city's population P_i, (i = A, B, C, D). As the population of each city increases, the production amount first increases and later decreases; the variation of the production amount is generated by the works of internal and external economies and diseconomies in each city. The relationship between a city's population and its production amount is different between the cities because they have different production environments. Figure 6.5a describes each city's production function.

Each city's population $P_i{}^*$ that maximizes its production amount is obtained as follows;

$P_A{}^* = 12.5$, $P_B{}^* = 7.4$, $P_C{}^* = 8.0$, $P_D{}^* = 3.13$. Then, Fig. 6.5b shows the relationship between the city's population and production amount per capita. Each city's population $P_i{}^{**}$ that maximizes its production amount per capita is obtained as follows: $P_A{}^{**} = 6.25$, $P_B{}^{**} = 3.4$, $P_C{}^{**} = 1.33$, $P_D{}^{**} = 1.88$. These cities' populations are smaller than those that maximize the production amount.

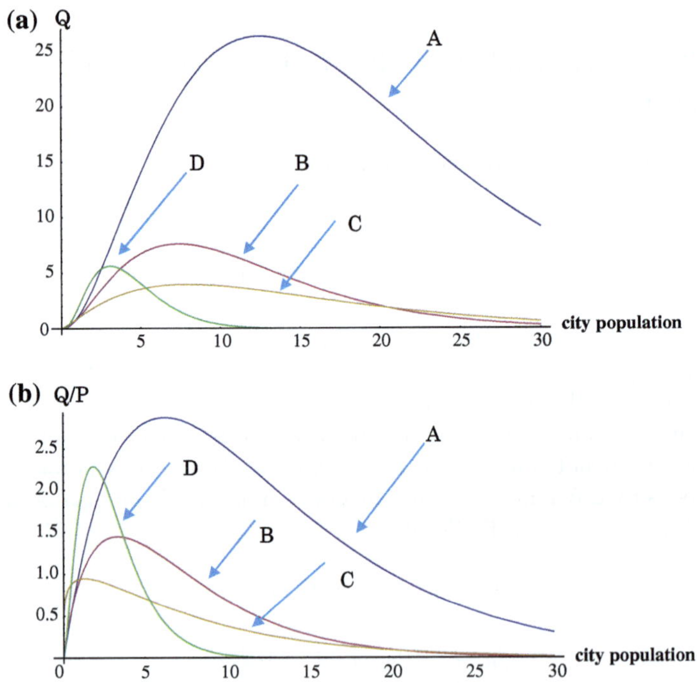

Fig. 6.5 The relationship between city's **a** population and production amount and **b** population and amount per capita

6.2.2 *Change of Optimal Population Size Due to an Increase of a Region's Population*

In this section, an assumption is added: the region where the four cities are located has population *T*, and this region's population is distributed between the four cities. This section analyzes how the region's population should be distributed to each city in order to maximize the region's production amount, TQ, which is produced by the four cities.[6] The optimal population of each of the cities can be derived by using the Lagrange Eq. (6.3).

$$\mathrm{TQ} = Q_{\mathrm{A}} + Q_{\mathrm{B}} + Q_{\mathrm{C}} + Q_{\mathrm{D}} - \lambda_{\mathrm{C}}(T - (P_{\mathrm{A}} + P_{\mathrm{B}} + P_{\mathrm{C}} + P_{\mathrm{D}})) \tag{6.3}$$

The optimal population of each city can be obtained by solving the following simultaneous equation systems with respect to P_{i}, (i = A, B, C, D):

$$\partial TQ/\partial P_{\mathrm{i}} = 0 \quad (\mathrm{i} = \mathrm{A}, \mathrm{B}, \mathrm{C}, \mathrm{D}) \tag{6.4}$$

$$\partial \mathrm{TQ}/\partial \lambda = 0 \tag{6.5}$$

The optimal population of each city, $P_{\mathrm{i}}{}^{*}$(i = A, B, C, D), is derived by changing the region's population from 10 to 45 by an interval of 5 and then to 46, which is the highest population of the region. In the next section, selecting the three representative region populations of 10, 30, and 45, the population and production amount of each city are derived for the three region's populations.

6.2.2.1 Population and Production Amount of Cities in a Low-Population Region

Table 6.1 shows the population and production amount of each city when the region's population is low, *T* = 10. The ranking of the four cities in terms of population is given as A, D, B, and C in descending order; and the ranking of the cities in terms of production is the same as that of city population. As suggested by the production function of city D in Fig. 6.5a, city D is ranked high when the population of the region is low. In this case, the region's total production amount is 25.228.

Using the figures shown in Table 6.1, Fig. 6.6a, b show the distributions of the city's population and production amount, respectively. As shown in Fig. 6.6a, when the region's population is low, the population distribution between the cities is a polarization type—one large city and three small cities, with no medium city.

[6]The analysis of the optimal population distribution of cities considering the production side have been compiled many authors, such as Beckmann and McPherson (1970) and Suh (1991).

Table 6.1 Population and production of cities in low-population region ($T = 10$)

City	City's population and share	City's production amount and share
A	6.939 (69 %)	19.83 (79 %)
B	1.283 (13 %)	1.382 (6 %)
C	0.024 (0.2 %)	0.013 (0.05 %)
D	1.752 (1.9 %)	4.059 (16 %)

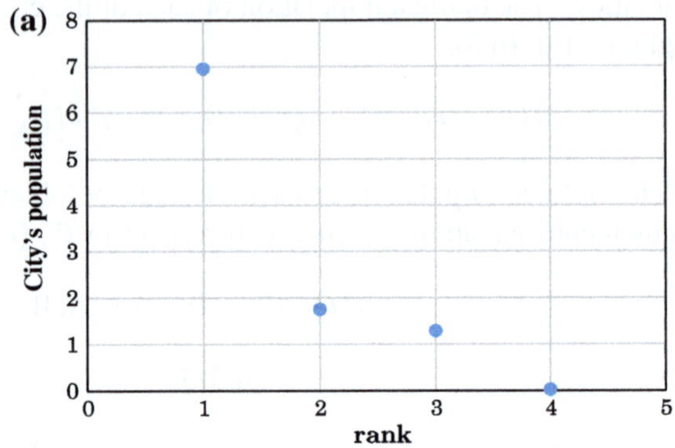

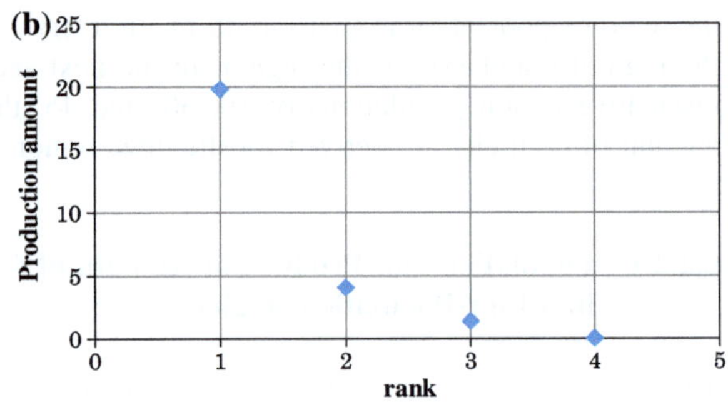

Fig. 6.6 **a** Population distribution of cities in low-population region. **b** Production amount distribution of cities in low-population region

As shown in Fig. 6.6b, when the region's population is low, the production amount distribution between the cities is also a polarization type—one large city and three small cities, with no medium city. When the region's population is low, the distribution patterns of population and the production amount between cities is the polarization type.

6.2.2.2 Population and Production Amount of Cities in a Medium-Population Region

Table 6.2 shows the population and production amount of each city when the region's population is at a medium level, $T = 30$. The ranking of cities in terms of population is given as A, B, D, and C in descending order; this ranking is different

Table 6.2 Population and production amount of cities in medium-population region ($T = 30$)

City	City's population and share	City's production amount and share
A	12.35 (41 %)	26.42 (60 %)
B	7.2 (24 %)	7.65 (18 %)
C	7.36 (25 %)	4 (9 %)
D	3.09 (10 %)	5.67 (13 %)

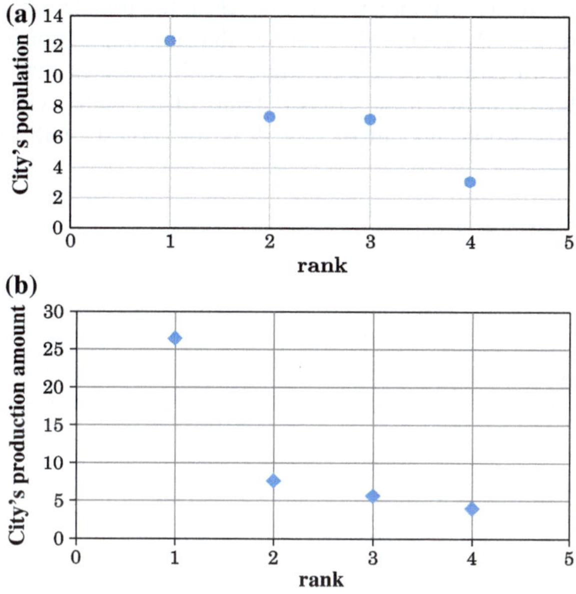

Fig. 6.7 **a** Population distribution of cities in a medium-population region. **b** Production distribution of cities in a medium-population region

from when the region's population is 10. The ranking of cities in terms of production is the order of city A, B, D, and C. In this case, the region's total production amount is 43.74.

Using the figures shown in Table 6.2, Fig. 6.7a, b show the distributions of the city's population and its production amount, respectively. As shown in Fig. 6.7a, when the region's population is at a medium level, $T = 30$, the population distribution between cities has a stratum—one large city, two medium cities, and one small city.

The production amount distribution between the cities is a polarization type—one large city and some small cities, with no medium city in terms of production amount. When the region's population is low, the distribution pattern of the production amount is a polarization type. Even if the region's population increases, the distribution of production amount remains the polarized pattern type.[7]

[7]As shown in a later section, when the region's population is 30, the total production amount in the region is maximized.

6.2.2.3 Population and Production Amount of Cities in a High-Population Region

Table 6.3 shows the population and production amount of each city when the region's population is at a high level, $T = 45$. The rank of cities in terms of population is given as C, A, B, and D in descending order; this city ranking is different from those when the region's population is 10 and 30. The rank of cities in terms of production is the order of A, B, D, and C. As indicated by Table 6.3, when the region's population is increased, the population of city C rises to overtake that of city A. Figure 6.8a shows that the population distribution pattern turns to a downward straight line. Figure 6.8b indicates that the production amount distribution between the cities remains of the same type, a polarized distribution. The production amount of city A is the largest of the four cities. City A keeps the

Table 6.3 Population and production amount of cities in high-population region ($T = 45$)

City	City's population and share	City's production amount and share
A	13.04 (29 %)	26.39 (64 %)
B	8.15 (18 %)	7.59 (18 %)
C	20.57 (44 %)	1.83 (4 %)
D	3.25 (7 %)	5.66 (14 %)

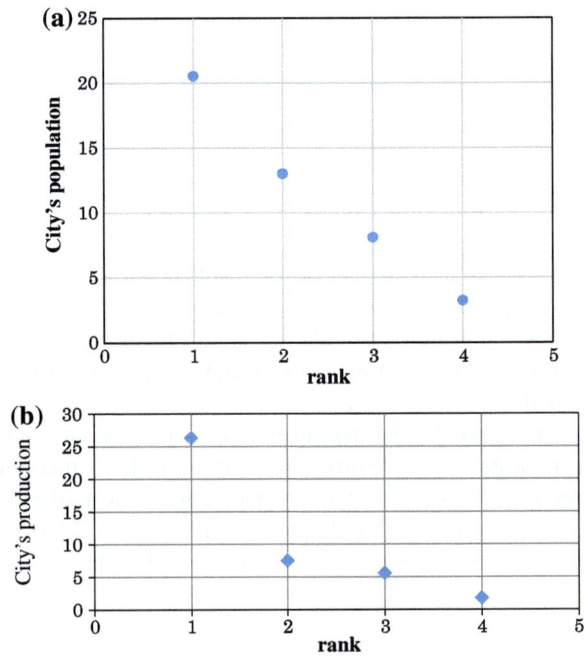

Fig. 6.8 **a** Population distribution of cities in a high-population region. **b** Production distribution of cities in a high-population region

highest rank in terms of production amount. On the contrary, the production amount of city C, which has the highest population, is ranked lowest. The above analysis clarifies that rankings in terms of population and production amount change according to a region's population. In this case, the region's production amount is 41.52.

6.2.2.4 The Relationship Between Population Distributions and the Production of Cities

It is shown in the above analysis that the distribution pattern of a city's population changes from a polarized pattern to a distribution with stratum and then to a straight line according to an increase of a region's population. The distribution pattern of a city's production amount is always a polarized pattern; it does not change according to an increase of the region's population. The reason that these distribution patterns are generated is explained as follows: on the basis of the production functions of the cities, each city's population is varied in order to maximize the total amount produced in the region. When the region's population is 10, city A attracts a large number of the region's population since the city A's production function can fully exercise production power. Thus, in this situation, the population distribution becomes a polarized pattern.

When the region's population is increased to 30, which is the population to archive the maximum production amount of the region, the populations of city B and C increase because these cities start to contribute to increase the total region's production and city A's marginal production power relatively decreases. Thus, in this situation, the population distribution becomes a pattern with stratum. The distribution of the production amount of cities maintains the type of polarization to achieve the maximum production quantity in a given region's population. It is noteworthy in this situation that although the city C has a share of 25 % of the region's population, it contributes to 9 % of the region's production quantity.

When the region's population is raised to 45, the population of city C greatly increases and its rank in terms of population becomes the highest; city A is ranked second. The reason for this change is explained as follows. When the region's population is at a high level beyond the level that achieves the maximum production amount in the region's production capacity, in order to utilize the superior production function of city A as much as possible, the population of city C should be increased because the production power of city C does decrease with the smallest rate as the region's population increases. As a result, the population distribution becomes a downward straight line in order not to decrease the production amount by an increase of a region's population. The distribution of the production amount of the cities maintains the type of polarization to achieve the maximum production quantity in a given region's population.

Because this analysis is conducted under the assumption that each city's population is determined to maximize the region's production amount, it is considered that distribution patterns derived in this analysis are the optimal ones from the principle of the maximization of a region's production amount. This study may shed light on the analysis of the change of ranking of cities in terms of the population and production amounts in the real world.

6.2.3 *Changes of a City System Due to an Increase of the Region's Population*

6.2.3.1 Change of a Region's Production Amount Due to an Increase of Its Population

Figure 6.9 describes the change of a production amount of the region as the region's population increases from 10 to 45 by an interval of 5 and then to 46, which is the upper boundary for the calculation method used here. As shown in Fig. 6.9, the production amount is increased as the region's population increases to 30. As the population increases beyond the population of 30, the production amount of the region starts to decrease due to the work of the diseconomies of agglomeration of each city.

6.2.3.2 The Population Change of Cities Due to an Increase of the Region's Population

Figure 6.10a–d show the change of population of the individual cities as the region's population increases. As shown by these figures, cities A, B, and D increase their population as the region's population increases to 40. Then, as the region's population increases beyond 40, their population decreases, while city C increases its population irrelative to the level of the region's population.

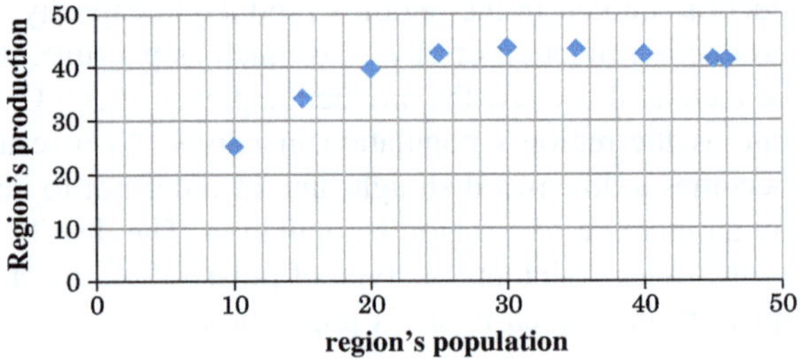

Fig. 6.9 Change of the production amount of the region as the region's population increases

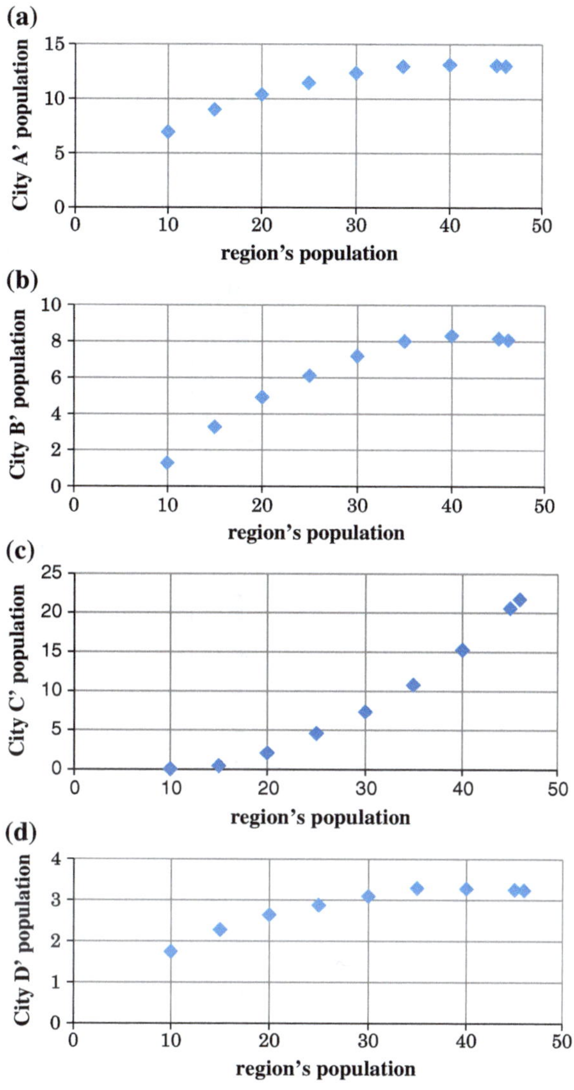

Fig. 6.10 Population change of cities A–D due to increase of region's population

6.2.3.3 Production Change of Cities Due to an Increase of the Region's Population

Figure 6.11a–d show the changes of the production amount of the individual cities as the region's population increases. As shown by these figures, cities A, B, and D increase their production amounts as the region's population increases to 40, and their amounts decrease as the region's population increases beyond 40. While city C increases its amount as the region's population increases to 30, its amount decreases when the region's population increases over 30.

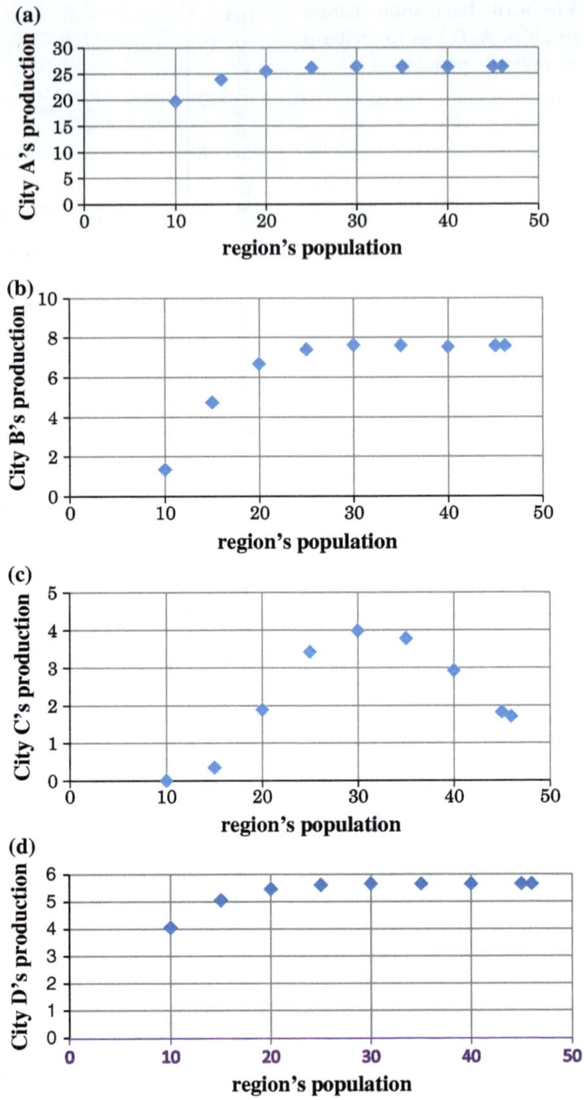

Fig. 6.11 Production change of cities A–D due to increase of region's population

As elucidated in the above analysis, as the region's population increases beyond the optimal level of the region's production capacity, $T = 30$, the population of the region is distributed between the cities to utilize the superior production function of city A. Thus, city A does not attract population in order to not decrease its production power as the region's population increases beyond 40. City C takes a larger share of the region's population because its production function slowly loses its production power as the city's population increases.

6.2.4 *Population Distribution Within a City System in Sweden*

It is inferred from the above analysis that while the region's population is low, a city with a superior production function attracts more population than other cities. Thus, the population distribution is a polarized pattern. As the region's population is increased to a medium level, some cities start to raise the region's production amount. The population distribution becomes a distribution with stratum. Then, the region's population increases beyond its optimal level in terms of the production capacity of the region. Cities whose production functions are not heavily affected by diseconomies of scale increase their population to achieve the highest production level possible. In this case, the population distribution may turn out to be a downward straight line.

Observing the population distributions of three Swedish counties in 2005, similar distribution patterns to those described in above analysis are found in the population distributions of the counties.[8] Figure 6.12a shows the municipality's population distribution in Jämtland County, of which population size is small; its population is 127,020. The population distribution is a polarized pattern. Figure 6.12b shows the municipality's population distribution in Scäne County, of which population size is large; its population is 1,184,500. The distribution of population is a pattern with stratum. This county has a city system that consists of one large city, three medium cities, and 29 small cities.

Figure 6.12c shows the municipality's population distribution in Halland County, which has a medium population size; the population is 288,859, which corresponds to 24 % of Scäne County's population; its area is 5462 km^2, which is 23 % of that of Scäne County. The distribution of population is a downward straight line. This county ranks ninth in terms of gross regional products of Sweden. Its GRP per capita is ranked at 18th in Sweden. Although a detailed analysis of the relationships between the city system and social and economic activities of this county is not conducted here, it is considered that two counties, Scäne County and Västra Götaland County, exist at both sides of this county, and their economic activities are large enough to attract laborers from Halland County. Halland County's population is relatively too large to operate efficiently the production activity compared to the production capacity of the county. This might be a reason that the population distribution between the municipalities reveals a downward straight line. Considering the compatibility of the population distributions of these three counties with those derived from the simulation analysis, it may be said that the analysis of the distribution of the municipality's population in counties of Sweden may provide an interesting insight about the city systems in terms of population and economic activities.

[8]In this analysis, Gotland County (an island county) is omitted.

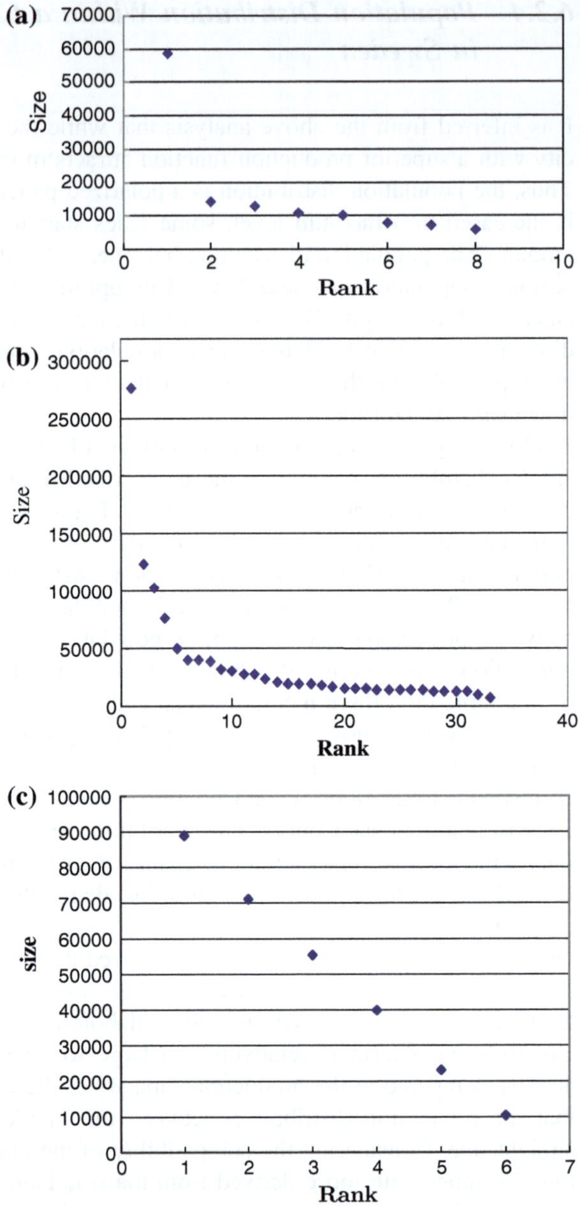

Fig. 6.12 Population distribution of municipalities in **a** Jämtland County (2005), **b** Scäne County (2005), **c** Halland County (2005). *Source* Swedish statistics

6.3 Change of a City System in the Real World

This section examines how city systems changed in the real world in the 1990s. The examination was conducted by using Japanese and Swedish data from the manufacturing industry, the retail industry, and populations. To advance this analysis, first, a hypothesis of the change of a city system is established from the viewpoints of the above two industries; then, the hypothesis is tested by the empirical analysis.

6.3.1 *Polarization of a City System by a Change in the Manufacturing Industry*

In the 1990s, the manufacturing industry concentrated their factories in a few territories to enjoy agglomeration economies and utilized large-scale infrastructure. As shown in the preceding chapter, the recent economic globalization forces many manufacturing firms to fragment their production processes and scatter them over local areas to reduce their production costs. As the fragmented processes depart from the existing agglomerations, which form a significant economic foundation of large and medium cities, the large and medium cities in industrial areas decay in the sector of the manufacturing activity. In particular, they cause serious social and economic damage to medium cities that cannot change the existing industrial composition by introducing advanced manufacturing factories to develop a new economic activity. As a result, economic globalization alters the firms' production pattern to squeeze the production activity of the medium cities and makes the city system polarized.

6.3.2 *Polarization of a City System by a Change of the Retail Industry*

The market areas of large retailers, such as department stores, become larger and larger as the transportation cost decreases. The expansion of these retailers' market areas alters not only the location pattern of these retailers but also the retailing structure of the city system in a region. If the market areas of large retailers must be expanded to maintain their retail operations, the retailers in large cities can enlarge their market areas with relative ease to obtain the necessary market area size because large cities have some ways to attract potential customers from the large surrounding area. However, large retailers in medium cities have difficulty enlarging their market areas because medium cities do not have the same the potential attraction power as large cities; thus, it is relatively difficult for large retailers in medium cities to secure the necessary market area size. They are exposed to the risk of decreasing the retail function to deal with more daily commodities. Because large retailers play a representative role in the tertiary sector of these cities, the decay of these retailers seriously damages the retail activity in middle-sized cities. Due to the decay of these cities, many city systems are composed of a large city providing a variety of goods, and many small cities deal with daily goods; the city systems tend to be polarized by a change of retail activities.

6.3.3 A Simple Test of the Hypothesis of a Polarized City System in a Country

It is possible to establish a hypothesis that because economic globalization weakens the manufacturing and retail activity in medium-sized cities, many city systems are polarized and are composed of a few large and diversified cities and many small and simplified cities.

To test this hypothesis, assuming that a country is covered by a large single city system, this section examines how the medium cities' shares of the labors of the manufacturing and retail industries and population declined in the period that globalization greatly proceeded. In this examination, the data of Japan and Sweden in the 1990s[9] are used.

6.3.4 Reduction of Medium Cities' Shares of Laborers and Population in 1990s

6.3.4.1 Reduction of Economic Activity and Population in Medium Cities in Japan

Let us examine the reduction of the medium cities' shares of the manufacturing labors in Japan. This analysis is conducted as follows. There were 659 cities in Japan as of 1990. The share of the number of the laborers in the manufacturing sector of a city was derived for 659 cities. In turn, the ranking of the city is carried out at order with a large share. The same procedures were taken as of 2002. Then, the variation or the percentage of the variation of the share of each ranked city between 1990 and 2002 was derived.

Figure 6.13 illustrates the variation of the share of each ranked city in the range from the 15th to the 240th. The rank of the cities that decrease the share is confined to between the 28th and the 97th. It is obvious that the medium cities, which are in the second rank group in the city system, decrease in the share of the manufacturing laborers.

Figure 6.14 covers all cities in Japan. It shows the percentage of the share variation of each ranked city. At a rank lower than the 98th, there is no city that decreases the share, and a lower-rank city leads to a higher positive percentage of the variation. It is obvious that all small cities less than 98th raise the activity standard in the manufacturing industry. The cities ranked in the largest city group lose the share.

---

[9]The data from Japan were provided by the data book (Toyo Keizai 2002) and the census of Japan (Statistics Bureau, Ministry of Public Management in Japan 1990 and 2000). The data from Sweden were provided by Statistics Sweden.

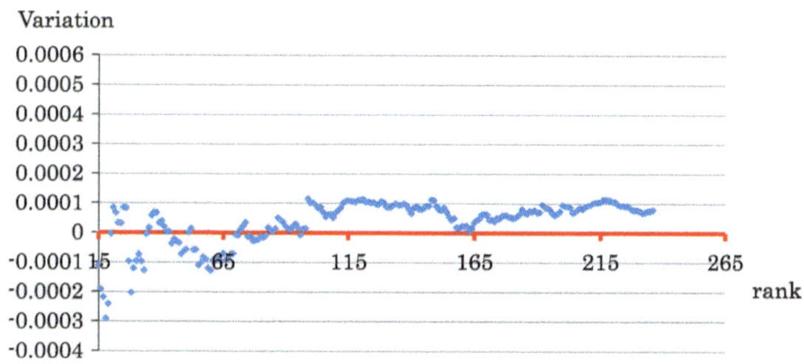

Fig. 6.13 Decrease in the medium cities' shares of manufacturing labor

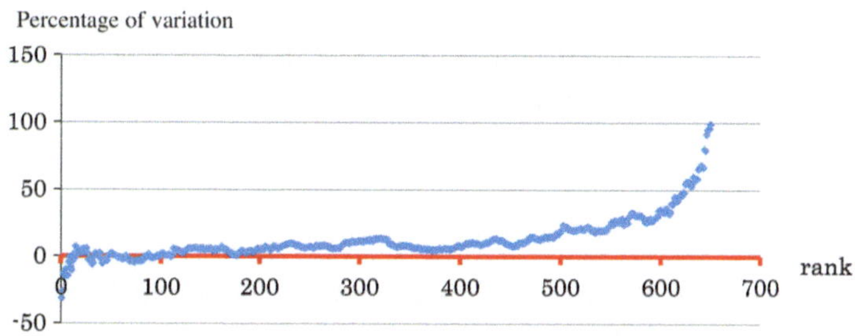

Fig. 6.14 Percentage of the variation of shares of manufacturing labor

The percentage of the variation of each ranked city's share of the retail workers is shown by Fig. 6.15. It illustrates that many cities with share decreases are in between the 23 and the 120th; there is no city that decreases the share in the range lower than the 238th. It can be said that the medium cities lose workers in the retail sector as well as the manufacturing.

Then, the variation of each ranked city's population share is inquired. Figure 6.16 shows the percentage of the increase and the decrease of the population

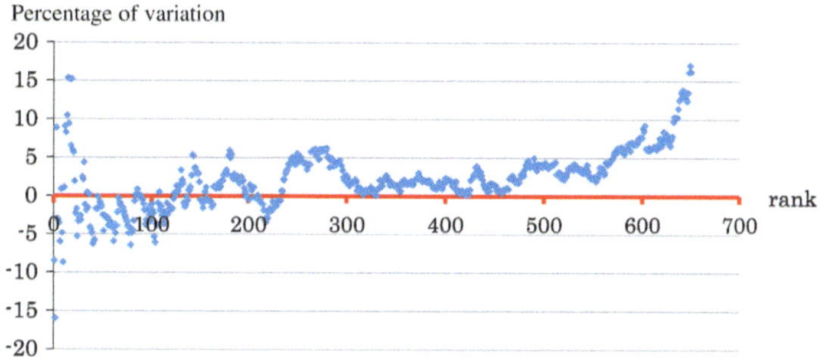

Fig. 6.15 Decrease in the medium cities' shares of retail workers

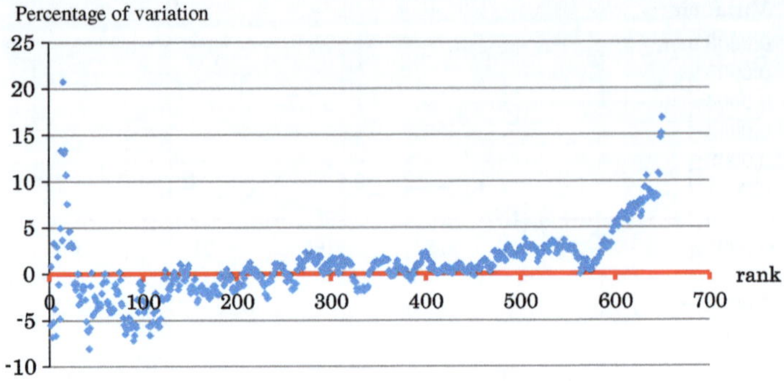

Fig. 6.16 Decrease in the middle cities' shares of population

shares of the cities. There are 191 cities with share decreases in between the 15th to the 250th. There is no city with share decreases in the range lower than the 388th. It is thus obvious that the middle-sized cities tend to decrease in the share of population.

6.3.4.2 Reduction of Economic Activity and Population in Medium Cities in Sweden

Let us examine the reduction of the middle-sized municipalities' shares of the laborers in the producing sector in the 1990s in Sweden. Figure 6.17 illustrates the variation of the share of each ranked municipality from the 50th to 289th. Figure 6.17 does not cover the range from the 1st to 49th because the variations of the large municipalities are too high to show them in this figure. Many of the municipalities that decrease in the share are in between the 70th and the 228th. In particular, the municipalities from the 100th to the 150th substantially decrease

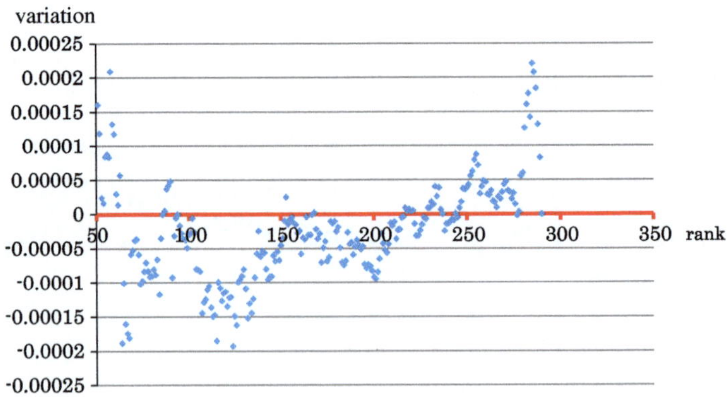

Fig. 6.17 Decrease in medium cities' shares of laborers in the secondary sector in Sweden

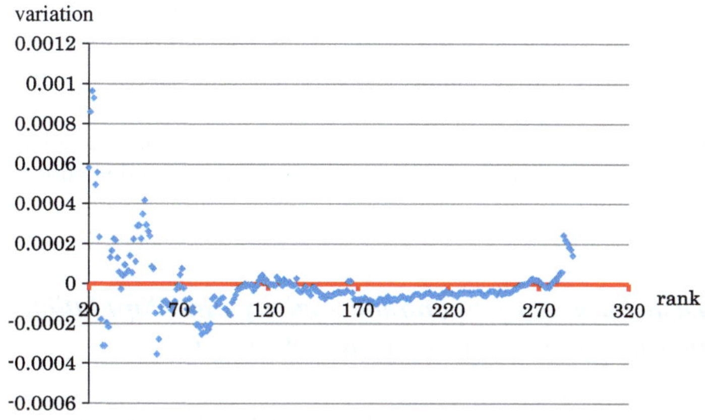

Fig. 6.18 Decrease in the medium cities' shares of workers in the tertiary sector

their shares. While there are 24 municipalities that increase in the shares in the range higher than the 29th, small municipalities lower than 230th also increase their shares. It is said that the medium municipalities greatly decrease the share of the production workers.

Figure 6.18, which covers the rank range from the 20th to 289th, illustrates the variation of each ranked municipality's share of workers in the tertiary sector. The municipalities with shares decrease belong to the range between the 60th and the 240th. The decrease of the shares of the municipality ranked from 57th to 110th are relatively large compared with others. Many large municipalities increase their shares, and some of the municipalities between the 115th and the 132nd also increase in their shares. It can be said that the medium municipalities lose the share of the workers in the tertiary industry. However, the variation trend of the tertiary sector in the range from the 100th to the 150th is the opposite of that of the producing sector.

Finally, the variation of each ranked municipality's population share is inquired. Figure 6.19 shows the variation of the shares of the municipalities which are in between the 50th and 289th. All municipalities from the 71st to the 270th reduce in

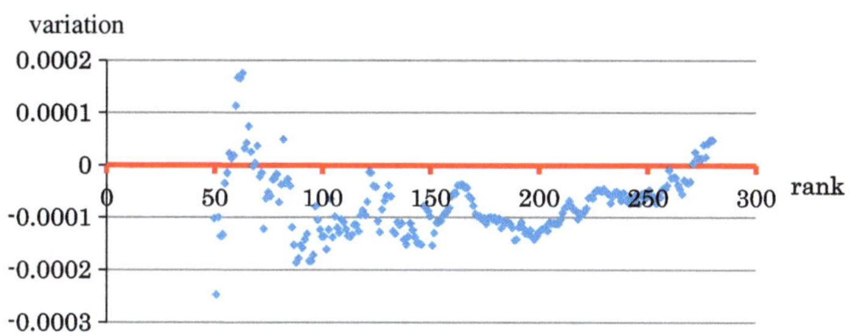

Fig. 6.19 Decrease in the middle cities' shares of population

the shares. In particular, the municipalities in the range between the 71st and the 117th substantially decrease in the shares of the population compared with other municipalities. There are 28 municipalities in the rank larger than the 50th that increase the share of population All the municipalities ranked lower than the 271st. increase in the share. It is clarified from the examination of the variations of the municipalities' shares of population that the middle-sized municipalities reduce the share of population.

6.3.5 Distributions of Economic Activity and Population in City Systems in Japan and Sweden

When a country is covered by a single city system, it is shown that the medium cities of Japan and Sweden tend to lose their economic activities and their population shares were reduced in the 1990s. There are 47 prefectures in Japan and there is a city system in each prefecture. Also, there is a city system in each county in Sweden.

Therefore, it is necessary for the understanding of the economic tendency of the second largest cities in a country to analyze the distributions of economic activities and population of cities in each region. Hence, this section inquires the extent to which the distributions of the economic activities and the population of the cities in a region are biased toward the largest city in the region in 1990s; also, it clarifies how a city system of each region is polarized or leveled between the cities in Japan and Sweden. This question is examined by using the coefficient of convergence, CD. The quotient of convergence is measured by the value of the divergence of the distribution of the laborers and the population of the city toward the labor and population of the largest city within the city system. The method for deriving the coefficient of convergence CD is explained in Sect. 8.2.2.

6.3.5.1 Distributions of Economic Activity and Population in City Systems in Japan

Let us examine how the city system of each region are polarized or how the city system is leveled between the cities in terms of the economic activity and the population in Japan and Sweden. First, the case of Japan is examined.

There are 47 prefectures in Japan. It is safe to say that a city system is laid in a prefecture. It is possible to classify 24 prefectures into the existing industrial area and the other 22 to the local area from the viewpoint of the manufacturing activity. (Because Okinawa prefecture is an isolated island, it is excluded in this examination.) The industrial prefectures are shown by the black painted area in Fig. 6.20.

The distribution change of the laborers and population in the city system is examined by the quotient of convergence, CD. A lower quotient implies that the distribution is more converged toward the largest city, whereas a higher coefficient means that the distribution becomes more level between the cities in a city system.

Fig. 6.20 Existing industrial regions and local regions in Japan

The analysis is conducted as follows. First, the values of CD for the labor distributions of the manufacturing and the retailing industry and also the values of the population are obtained for 46 prefectures as of 1990 and 2002. Second, the *three average* CD values of them in the industrial area and the local area as of 1990 and 2002 are derived, respectively. Third, a comparison of the three average values at the two different years shows the change direction of the distributions in the industrial area and the local area, converging toward the largest city or leveling between the cities. Table 6.4 illustrates the three average values of CD in the two areas as well as the change directions of the distributions in the two areas in the 1990s.

From the figures shown in Table 6.4, the following were found for each of the two industry sectors and populations in Japan:

(1) The manufacturing factories diffuse from the large cities in the existing industrial area to the neighboring small cities in this area and disperse to the relatively large cities in the local area. As a result, the manufacturing labor distribution is leveled in many city systems in the existing industrial area. In many city systems in the local area, the distribution converges toward the largest city. Furthermore, it is interesting that the value of CD in local area becomes higher than that of the existing industrial area in the 1990s.

(2) The retail sector in the small cities in the existing industrial area raises the activity standard, while that of the large cities relatively falls. Thus, the distribution of the retail workers in many city systems in the existing industrial area has a tendency to become level. The distribution change of the retailing workers in the local area is evenly divided in two ways: converging and leveling.

Table 6.4 Change of distributions of economic activities and population in Japan

Manufacturing sector	Existing industrial area	Local area
Average CD in 1992	0.6096	0.6327
Average CD in 2002	0.6355	0.6305
Variation of Av. CD	+0.0258	−0.0022
Number of prefecture, leveling	20	9
Number of prefecture, converging	4	13
Retailing sector		
Average CD in 1991	0.5363	0.5298
Average CD in 2002	0.5426	0.5374
Variation of Av. CD	+0.0063	+0.0077
Number of prefecture, leveling	16	10
Number of prefecture, converging	8	12
Population		
Average CD in 1991	0.5531	0.5569
Average CD in 2002	0.5605	0.5543
Variation of Av. CD	+0.007	−0.003
Number of prefecture, leveling	18	9
Number of prefecture, converging	6	13

(3) The population distribution of the many city systems in the local area converges toward the largest city, while in the industrial area the distribution has a tendency to be level. The trends in the distribution are almost the same as those of the manufacturing industry.

6.3.5.2 Distributions of Economic Activity and Population in City Systems in Sweden

Let us inquire about the changes of the municipalities' shares of the number of the two kinds of employment and population in the 1990s in Sweden. There are 21 counties in Sweden (since Gotland is an isolated island, it is excluded in this examination). A city system is laid in each county. Of all counties, 13 are classified into the existing industrial area and other 7 counties to the local area. The industrial counties are continuously located in the southern part of Sweden, as shown by Fig. 6.21.

Table 6.5 shows the three average values of CD in the industrial area and the local one, as well as the change directions of the distributions in the industrial area and the local areas in Sweden. The following facts were found for each of the two industries and population.

(1) The production activities diffuse from the large municipalities in the industrial area to the neighboring small municipalities in this area or disperse to the

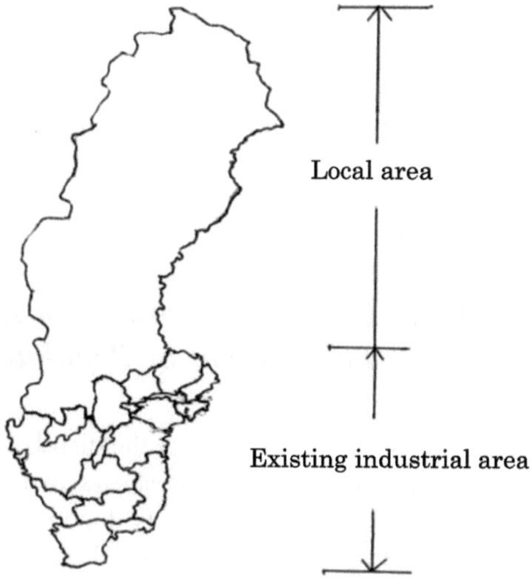

Fig. 6.21 Industrial area and local area in Sweden

Table 6.5 Change of distributions of economic activities and population in Sweden

Secondary sector	Existing industrial area	Local area
Average CD in 1990	0.6012	0.5847
Average CD in 2000	0.6078	0.5815
Variation of Av. CD	+0.0066	−0.0032
Number of county, leveling	9	2
Number of county, converging	4	5
Tertiary sector		
Average CD in 1990	0.4596	0.4932
Average CD in 2000	0.4596	0.4828
Variation of Av. CD	0	−0.0104
Number of county, leveling	7	1
Number of county, converging	6	6
Population		
Average CD in 1990	0.5722	0.6800
Average CD in 2000	0.5640	0.6017
Variation of Av. CD	−0.0082	−0.078
Number of county, leveling	3	2
Number of county converging	10	5

relatively large municipalities in the local area. This trend is the same as that of Japan. In addition, the production activity in Sweden is more concentrated at the large municipalities than Japanese ones.

(2) The tertiary industry in the city systems in the local area becomes more concentrated at large municipalities; that of the industrial area does not change but maintains the status quo.

(3) The population distributions converge toward the large municipalities in many city systems in both the industrial area and the local area. The trend that the distribution of population in the existing industrial area converges toward the large municipalities is different from the Japanese one.

6.3.6 Results of the Inspection of the Hypothesis of Polarization of Population

A simple empirical analysis of the distributions of the laborers and the population in Japan and Sweden in 1990s shows that (1) the economic activities of the many middle-sized cities are relatively depressed, while some of the large cities and many of the small cities relatively raise their activity level. It is therefore said that due to the economic decay of the medium cities, the distributions of the economic activity and the population in regions become divided into two parts—a large city and many small cities. (2) The distributions of the economic activities and the population become relatively converged toward the largest city in the local areas in both Japan and Sweden. On the other hand, the distribution change of the population in the existing industrial area is different between Japan and Sweden. The distribution of the population in the existing industrial area in Japan becomes leveled among the cities, while that of Sweden becomes converged toward the large cities.

Although there are some different changes in the distribution patterns between the two countries, the results from the simple empirical analysis confirm the proposed hypothesis that as globalization makes progress, the distributions of the economic activity and the population within the city systems become polarized, with a few of the large cities and many small cities.

Chapter 7
Analysis of a City System by Using Cities' Land Rents

This chapter analyzes the interactions of economic activities of individual cities in a city system from the viewpoint of the land rents of the cities' areas. The analysis of the land rents of the city area may contribute to an understanding of the relationships between the cities' economic activities within a city system. The land rent analysis may deepen the comprehension of the economic activity of the city system by complementing the city systems built on the basis of the retailers' market areas: The city systems built by using the market areas are not appropriate to examine the mechanisms of the reciprocal economic activities between the cities within a city system, and it is difficult to analyze the effects of the economic changes in a city on other cities. This chapter may shed the light on the analysis of the reciprocal economic influences between the cities and the effects of the economic changes in a city on other cities within a city system.[1]

7.1 Assumptions and Framework of the Analysis

Let us assume that there is a city system in a region that consists of *n* different sized cities. The spatial structure of each city is assumed to be a linear structure. Figure 7.1 describes the city's spatial structure: The territory of each city is shown by the length of a straight line. A market for the final goods produced by the manufacturing firms in the city area is at the west end of the line, which is shown by a small circle point, M. There is a business district that is bordered by the market. This district area is illustrated by a bold line from the market stretched toward the east end of the business district, denoted by U_L. Then, the area where the manufacturing firms are located extends from point U_L to the east end of the city area, U_H. This area is shown by the thin line in Fig. 7.1. The values of U_L and U_H are

[1]Kozu (1998) analyzed the land rent distribution within a city system, incorporating the agglomeration economies into consideration.

T. Ishikawa, *Dynamic Locational Phases of Economic Activity in the Globalized World*, DOI 10.1007/978-981-10-0524-4_7

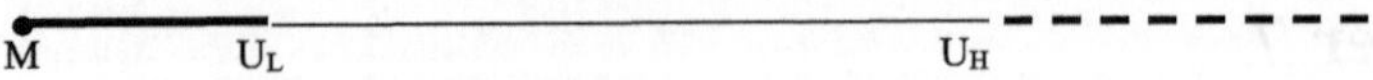

Fig. 7.1 A linear city and its spatial structure

different between the cities. From the end of the city, point U_H, agricultural land is developed, which is represented by the dotted line in Fig. 7.1. The n individual cities are away from each other.

The manufacturing firms transport the produced goods from their location to the market point M. The price of the goods in the market is given by P. Thus, the revenue of a manufacturing firm, R, is given by Eq. (7.1):

$$R = (P - tu)Q \tag{7.1}$$

Here, t is the freight rate of the goods, u is the distance from the market to the firm's location, and Q is the production amount, which also denotes the sales quantity in the market. Firms produce the goods by capital K and land L. Their production function is represented by Eq. (7.2):

$$Q = \left(\alpha K^{-\beta} + (1-\alpha)L^{-\beta}\right)^{-1/\beta} \tag{7.2}$$

where α and β are positive parameters. The firm's cost function is given by Eq. (7.3):

$$C = iK + r(u)L + tuQ \tag{7.3}$$

where i is the interest rate and $r(u)$ indicates the land rent to the firm, which is away from the market by distance u. The firm's profit Y is shown by Eq. (7.4):

$$Y = R - C \tag{7.4}$$

For simplicity, it is assumed that each firm occupies one unit land. The value of K/L is denoted by k and Q/L is denoted by q.

Let us analyze the firm's profit per unit length, y. The values of q and y are given by Eqs. (7.5) and (7.6), respectively.

$$\mathrm{q} = \left(\alpha k^{-\beta} + (1-\alpha)\right)^{-1/\beta} \tag{7.5}$$

$$y = P\left(\alpha k^{-\beta} + (1-\alpha)\right)^{-1/\beta} - r(u) - ik - tu\left(\alpha k^{-\beta} + (1-\alpha)\right)^{-1/\beta} \tag{7.6}$$

Equation (7.6) is transformed to Eq. (7.7):

$$y = (P - tu)\left(\alpha k^{-\beta} + (1-\alpha)\right)^{-1/\beta} - r(u) - ik \tag{7.7}$$

Using Eq. (7.7), the optimal location and value of k are derived by solving simultaneous Eqs. (7.8) and (7.9), respectively:

$$\mathrm{d}y/\mathrm{d}u = -r'(u) - t\left(\alpha k^{-\beta} + (1-\alpha)\right)^{-1/\beta} = 0 \tag{7.8}$$

$$\mathrm{d}y/\mathrm{d}k = -i + (P - tu)q\alpha k^{-\beta}/\left(k\left(\alpha k^{-\beta} + (1-\alpha)\right)\right) = 0 \tag{7.9}$$

where $r'(u)$ means d$r(u)$/du. Firms are assumed to be under competition. In the competitive equilibrium, Eq. (7.10) is established:

$$y = (P - tu)\left(\alpha k^{-\beta} + (1-\alpha)\right)^{-1/\beta} - r(u) - ik = 0 \tag{7.10}$$

From Eqs. (7.8) and (7.9), $r'(u)$ is shown by Eq. (7.11):

$$r'(u) = -ikt\left(\alpha k^{-\beta} + (1-\alpha)\right)/\left((P - tu)\alpha k^{-\beta}\right) \tag{7.11}$$

From Eq. (7.10), $r(u)$ is given by Eq. (7.12):

$$r(u) = (P - tu)q - ik \tag{7.12}$$

Using Eqs. (7.9) and (7.12), the land rent a firm bears is given by Eq. (7.13):

$$r(u) = ik(1-\alpha)/\alpha k^{-\beta} \tag{7.13}$$

From Eqs. (7.11) and (7.13), Eq. (7.14) can be derived:

$$r(u)'/r(u) = -t\left(\alpha k^{-\beta} + (1-\alpha)\right)/\left((P - tu)(1-\alpha)\right) \tag{7.14}$$

Let us integrate the both hands of Eq. (7.14) with respect to u from U_L to U_H as Eq. (7.15):

$$\int_{U_L}^{U_H} r'(u)/r(u)\mathrm{d}u = -S\int_{U_L}^{U_H} t/(P - tu)\mathrm{d}u \tag{7.15}$$

where $S = (\alpha k^{-\beta} + (1-\alpha))/(1-\alpha)$. From Eqs. (7.15), (7.16a) and (7.16b) are derived:

$$\mathrm{Log}(r(U_L)) - \mathrm{Log}(r(U_H)) = -S(\mathrm{Log}((P - tU_H)/(P - tU_L))) \tag{7.16a}$$

$$\mathrm{Log}(r(U_H)) = \mathrm{Log}(r(U_L)) + S(\mathrm{Log}((P - tU_H)/(P - tU_L))) \tag{7.16b}$$

If the land rent of the agricultural land is the same throughout a region, the land rents of the eastern point of each city's areas, which are bordered by agricultural land use, are the same. That is, the land rents at U_H of all the cities, which are given by Eq. (7.16b), are the same values.

7.2 Land Rent and Capital Amount in a City

7.2.1 Land Rent Distribution in a City Area

Let us suppose that the n cities within a city system are ordered by the length of its city area; the largest city is ranked 1 and the smallest city is ranked N. The larger city has larger U_L and U_H. The U_L and U_H of each city are shown by U_{iL} and U_{iH}, (i = 1, 2, 3, n … N). The price of the finished good of each city is denoted by P_i (i = 1, 2, 3, n … N)

Now, the relationship of the land rents at points U_{1L} and U_{1H} of the largest city and those of the city n are given by Eqs. (7.17) and (7.18), respectively:

$$\mathrm{Log}(r_1(U_{1L})) - \mathrm{Log}(r_1(U_{1H})) = -S(\mathrm{Log}((P_1 - t_1U_{1H})/(P_1 - t_1U_{1L}))) \quad (7.17)$$

$$\mathrm{Log}(r_n(U_{nL})) - \mathrm{Log}(r_n(U_{nH})) = -S(\mathrm{Log}((P_n - t_nU_{nH})/(P_n - t_nU_{nL}))) \quad (7.18)$$

Because the land rents at the eastern points of all the cities are the same, Eq. (7.19) is derived from Eqs. (7.17) and (7.18):

$$\begin{aligned}\mathrm{Log}(r_n(U_{nL})) &= \mathrm{Log}(r_1(U_{1L}))\\ &\quad + S(\mathrm{Log}((P_1 - t_1U_{1H})/(P_1 - t_1U_{1L})) - \mathrm{Log}((P_n - t_nU_{nH})/(P_n - t_nU_{nL})))\end{aligned} \quad (7.19)$$

Equation (7.19) indicates that the land rents at points U_{nL} of each area of cities ranked from the second to the smallest city depend on the land rent at the end point of the largest city, $r_1(U_{1L})$. In addition, it is known that if the land rent $r_n(U_{nL})$ is determined by Eq. (7.19), the land rent distribution in the city area can be shown by using Eq. (7.20):

$$\mathrm{Log}(r_n(u)) = \mathrm{Log}(r_n(U_{nL})) + S\,\mathrm{Log}((P_n - t_nu)/(P_n - t_nU_{nL})) \quad (7.20)$$

7.2.2 Capital Amount Used by Manufacturing Firms

Now, the firm's profit y is represented as Eq. (7.21):

$$y = (Pi - t_iu)q - \exp[\mathrm{Log}(r_n(u))] - ik \quad (7.21)$$

From Eqs. (7.9) and (7.21) is transformed to Eq. (7.22):

$$y = ik\left(\alpha k^{-\beta} + 1 - \alpha\right)/\alpha k^{-\beta} - \exp[\mathrm{Log}(r_n(u))] - ik \tag{7.22}$$

The firm's profit y is given by Eq. (7.23):

$$y = ik\left[k^{-\beta}\left(\alpha k^{-\beta} + 1 - \alpha\right)/\alpha - 1\right] - \exp[\mathrm{Log}(r_n(u))] \tag{7.23}$$

Because every firm's profit becomes zero in the competitive equilibrium, the amount capital per land of the firm located at distance u from the market is derived by solving Eq. (7.24) with respect to k.

$$\begin{aligned} y &= ik\left[k^{-\beta}\left(\alpha k^{-\beta} + 1 - \alpha\right)/\alpha - 1\right] - \exp[\mathrm{Log}(r_1(U_{1L}))] \\ &\quad + \left(\left(\alpha k^{-\beta} + 1 - \alpha\right)/(1 - \alpha)\right)[(\mathrm{Log}((P_1 - t_1 U_{1H})/(P_1 - t_1 U_{1L})) - \mathrm{Log}((P_n - t_n U_{nH})/(P_n - t_n U_{nL})))] = 0 \end{aligned} \tag{7.24}$$

Once the value of k is derived, the land rent and the production amount in every city area are obtained.

7.3 Analysis of Land Rents and Production Amounts of Cities Within a City System

This subsection concretely derives land rents, production amounts, and capital amounts in each city area, assuming that there are six different sized cities in a city system; numerical values are assigned to parameters as follows: $U_{1L} = 4$, $U_{1H} = 25$, $U_{2L} = 2.25$, $U_{2H} = 17.5$, $U_{3L} = 2$, $U_{3H} = 12.5$, $U_{4L} = 1.75$, $U_{4H} = 5$, $U_{5L} = 1.5$, $U_{5H} = 2$, $U_{6L} = 1.2$, $U_{6H} = 1.35$; $P_1 = 150$, $P_2 = 100$, $P_3 = 90$, $P_3 = 40$, $P_5 = 35$, $P_6 = 30$; $t_1 = 0.9$, $t_2 = t_3 = 0.5$, $t_4 = t_5 = t_6 = 0.1$; $\alpha = 0.8$, $\beta = 0.5$; lastly, the land rent of point U_{1L} of the largest city is given as $r_1(U_{1L})) = 3$.

Let us derive the land rents, production amounts, and capital amounts per land at points of U_L and U_H of each city. These values are derived from the above equations, and they are shown in Table 7.1. The distribution of the land rents at point U_L of each city is described in Fig. 7.2a. As shown in Table 7.1, the land rents and the values of other terms at the points U_H of all cities are the same. The land rents and values of other terms at points U_L of all the cities are different.

As the city size is smaller, the land rents at points U_L become lower. Figure 7.2b shows the distribution of the production amounts at point U_L of the cities. The firm's production amount at point U_L becomes larger as the city size becomes smaller.

The total production amounts, TQ, of each city can be approximately derived by using the production quantities at two points of U_L and U_H of each city. These quantities are shown in Fig. 7.2c. Because the largest city has the largest area where

Table 7.1 Land rent, production amount, and capital count of each city

Rank	t	$r(U_L)$	$r(U_H)$	$q(U_L)$	$q(U_H)$	$k(U_L)$	$k(U_H)$
1	0.9	3	1.0457	0.037	0.4301	0.025	0.3646
2	0.5	1.31	1.0457	0.1224	0.4301	0.0904	0.3646
3	0.5	1.257	1.0457	0.1981	0.4301	0.1526	0.3646
4	0.1	1.075	1.0457	0.4013	0.4301	0.3368	0.3646
5	0.1	1.051	1.0457	0.4251	0.4301	0.3598	0.3646
6	0.1	1.048	1.0457	0.4283	0.4301	0.3629	0.3646

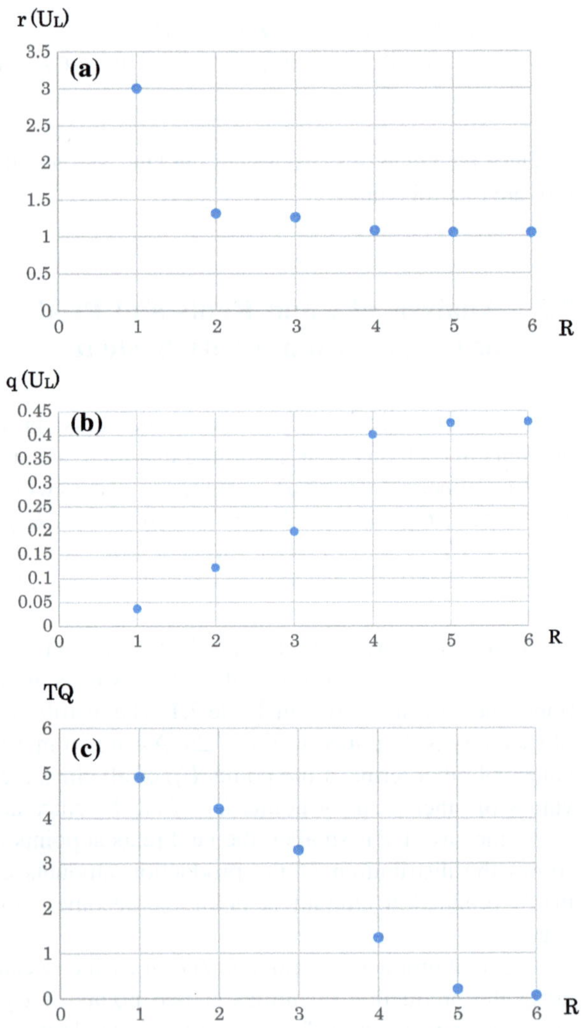

Fig. 7.2 **a** Distribution of the land rents at point U_L of the cities. **b** Distribution of production amounts per land at point U_L of the cities. **c** Distribution of total production amounts of cities

the manufacturing firms are located, the largest city produces the largest production amount. The distribution of the city's production amounts decreases smoothly according to the city's size rank.

7.4 Influences of Changes in Freight Rates and Production Efficiency on Cities

7.4.1 Effect of a Decrease of Freight Rate in the Largest City on Land Rent and Production

In this section, the freight rate in the largest city is reduced from 0.9 to 0.8, with other parameters remaining the same. Let us analyze the effect of a reduction of the freight rate in the largest city on the land rents and the production amounts of other cities. The method of analysis is the same as those of the previous analysis. The analysis results are presented in Table 7.2. Figure 7.3a shows a change of the distribution of land rents at point U_L of each city. Figure 7.3b depicts the change of the distribution of the production amount at point U_L of each city. From a comparison of Tables 7.1 and 7.2, it is known that a reduction of the freight rate of the largest city increases the land rents of other cities and decreases the production amounts of all the cities.

In Fig. 7.3a, the diamond indicators, which are almost hidden by the squares, show the land rent when the freight rate is 0.9; the squares show the land rent when the freight rate is 0.8. Figure 7.3a shows that the reduction of the freight rate slightly raises the land rents at point U_L of the cities ranked 4, 5, and 6 more than those of the cities ranked 2 and 3. This distribution of the land rent seems to be more clearly separated into two parts.

Figure 7.3b indicates that the reduction of the freight rate reduces the production amounts at point U_L of each city. In Fig. 7.3b, the diamonds show the production amount when the freight rate is 0.9 and the squares show the amount when the freight rate is 0.8. The reduction in the largest city makes the gap between the amounts at point U_L of the cities ranked 3 and 4 rather large. The distribution of production amounts are evenly divided into the two groups.

Table 7.2 The effects of a reducing freight rate in the largest city on other cities

Rank	t	$r(U_L)$	$r(U_H)$	$q(U_L)$	$q(U_H)$	$k(U_L)$	$k(U_H)$
1	0.8	3	1.1054	0.028	0.3705	0.019	0.3074
2	0.5	1.339	1.1054	0.0656	0.3705	0.046	0.3074
3	0.5	1.303	1.1054	0.1326	0.3705	0.099	0.3074
4	0.1	1.135	1.1054	0.3401	0.3705	0.2787	0.3074
5	0.1	1.111	1.1054	0.3655	0.3705	0.3024	0.3074
6	0.1	1.107	1.1054	0.3686	0.3705	0.3056	0.3074

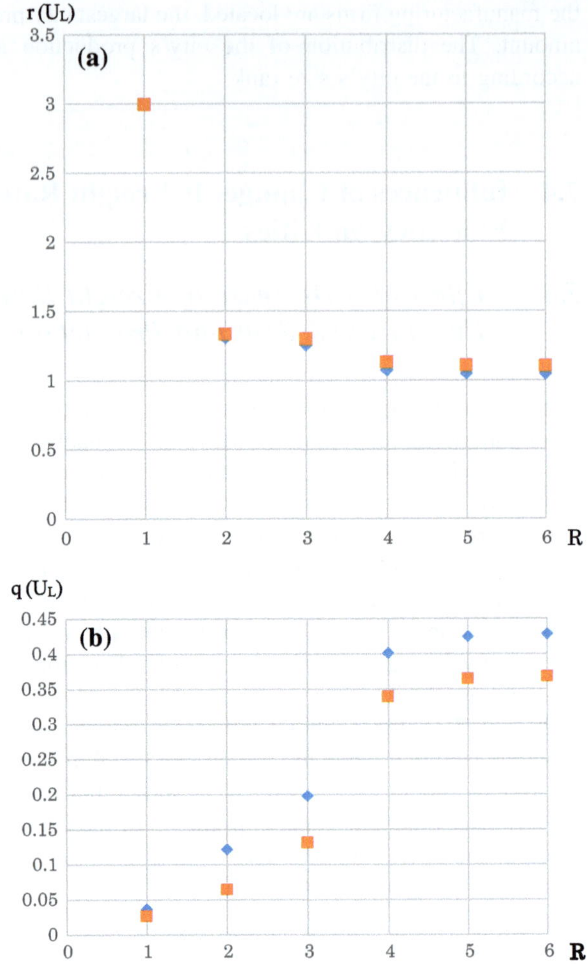

Fig. 7.3 Effects of the freight rate in the largest city on (**a**) land rents at point U_L of cities and (**b**) production at point U_L of cities

7.4.2 *Effects of Increasing Production Efficiency on Land Rent and Production*

In this section, the freight rate of the largest city is again assumed to be 0.9 and the parameter β is increased from 0.5 to 0.7. Other parameters' values are the same those of the previous analysis. This section examines the effects of increasing production efficiency on the land rents and production amounts at point U_L of cities. Table 7.3 shows the results of the calculations conducted by the same method. Figure 7.4a depicts the distribution change of the land rents at point $U_{L,}$ and Fig. 7.4b shows the distribution of the production amount at point U_L of all cities.

In Fig. 7.4a, the diamonds show the land rent when the parameter β is 0.5 and the squares show the land rent when the parameter β is 0.7. Figure 7.4a shows that

Table 7.3 Effects of production efficiency on the land rents and production of cities

Rank	β	$r(U_L)$	$r(U_H)$	$q(U_L)$	$q(U_H)$	$k(U_L)$	$k(U_H)$
1	0.7	3	1.1634	0.1663	0.6374	0.1315	0.5805
2	0.7	1.7633	1.1634	0.421	0.6374	0.3610	0.5805
3	0.7	1.5749	1.1634	0.4828	0.6374	0.4215	0.5805
4	0.7	1.2085	1.1634	0.6193	0.6374	0.5613	0.5805
5	0.7	1.1711	1.1634	0.6343	0.6374	0.5772	0.5805
6	0.7	1.1661	1.1634	0.6363	0.6374	0.5794	0.5805

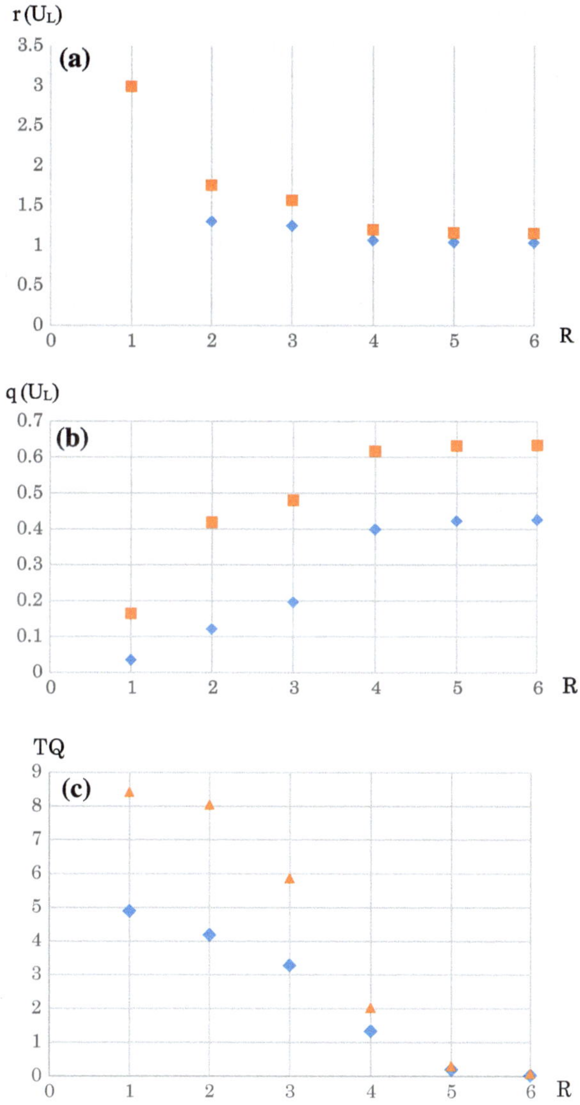

Fig. 7.4 Effects of production efficiency on the (**a**) land rent at point U_L of cities, (**b**) production amounts of at point U_L of cities, and (**c**) total production amounts of cities

the increase of the production efficiency raises the land rents at point U_L of the cities ranked second and third more than those of cities ranked fourth, fifth, and sixth; the increase of the production efficiency makes three layers in the distribution of the land rents at point U_L of each city. In Fig. 7.4b, the diamonds show the production amounts when the parameter β is 0.5 and the squares show the amounts when the parameter β is 0.7. Figure 7.4b indicates that the increase of β increases the production amounts at point U_L of each city. The increase of the production efficiency makes the gap between the production amounts at point U_L of the cities ranked first and second larger and makes the gap between the production amounts of the cities ranked third and fourth smaller. Consequently, the distribution of production amounts has three layers.

Figure 7.4c shows the effect of the increase of production efficiency on the total production amount of each city. The triangles indicate the total amount of each city when the value of β is increased to 0.7. The diamonds indicate the amounts when the value of β is 0.5. It is said that the increase of the production efficiency makes the distribution of the total production divide into two parts.

The land rent analysis developed here may contribute to the theory of the city system by the analysis of the reciprocal relationships between the cities within a city system. This analysis shows the mechanisms of influence of the change of the economic activity in the largest city on the land rents and the production amounts of the smaller cities. The following three results derived from the rent analysis may be interesting for regional governments:

(1) The reduction of the freight rate in the largest city's area decreases the production amounts of other smaller cities.
(2) An increase of the production efficiency of the firms increases the production amounts of all the cities.
(3) Changes in the freight rate and the production efficiency influence the distribution of the city's production amount within the city system in different ways.

These theoretical suggestions may be useful for the locational policy makers of regional governments that plan to reform the city system for regional economic development.

Chapter 8
City System as a Location Factor

8.1 Role of a City System in a Firm's Location Decision-Making

Suppose that a manufacturing firm has planned to establish a new factory and searches for the factory's location; then, it starts to set the location prospective area (LPA) within a large geographical space. In the process of the firm's region selections within the LPA, it may consider many location factors, such as the security level, educational institutions, and environment surrounding the possible location. This chapter proposes that the city systems in a region should be incorporated into the decision-making processes when determining a location. Because a city system influences the firm's performance as a whole, the effects of a city system on the firm are similar to that of the social infrastructure.

To verify that a city system is an important factor in a firm's location determination, this chapter clarifies that the city system in a region is related to the region's performance, which is revealed by the concept of social health. To achieve this end, using the data of Japan, this chapter shows the relationship between the structural characteristics of a city system and the social health achieved in the region according to the following three steps:

1. Derivation of the numerical index that reveals the structural characteristics of the city system
2. Estimation of the region's social health, being composed of several items
3. Examination of the relationships between the numerical indexes and the region's social health.

T. Ishikawa, *Dynamic Locational Phases of Economic Activity in the Globalized World*, DOI 10.1007/978-981-10-0524-4_8

8.2 Numerical Index of Characteristics of a City System

8.2.1 Derivation of the City System Index

The structural characteristics of a city system are examined from two points of view —the distribution of a city's population and the locations of cities in a region. A city system is characterized by these two terms of the city's population (CD) and the city's location pattern (SC). The City System Index, which is composed of CD and SC, characterizes numerically the city systems in a region.

8.2.2 Divergence of a City's Population Distribution Toward the Largest City

The coefficient of divergence (CD), which indicates the divergence of the population distribution toward the primary city in a region, is derived as follows (Sheppard 1982).

Assume there are N cities in a region. Let p_r denote the population share of a city, p_r, for the total city population in the region. Then, Eq. (8.1) is established:

$$1 = \sum_{r=1}^{N} p_r \tag{8.1}$$

If there is no a priori information on the cities, it is rational to infer that every city has the same share, $p_r = 1/N$. This inference is derived by maximizing Eq. (8.2) in the subject to Eq. (8.1):

$$H = -\sum_{r=1}^{N} p_r L_N(r) \tag{8.2}$$

In the real world, there is a priori information on the cities. Thus, let r indicates the rank of a city according to its population size, multiply the value of $L_N(r)$ by its share as a weight, and then sum up these values. Dividing by N gives Eq. (8.3). The value obtained by Eq. (8.3), CD, is considered as the coefficient of the divergence of the population distribution to the primary city in a region.

$$\text{CD} = (1/N)\sum_{r=1}^{N} p_r L_N(r) \tag{8.3}$$

If the population of the region is distributed equally between the cities, the coefficient of the divergence is given by Eq. (8.4):

$$\mathrm{CD} = N^{-2} \sum_{r=1}^{N} L_N(r) \tag{8.4}$$

The value of CD is used as an index that characterizes the distribution of a city's population within a city system. As the distribution of the city's population starts to diverge toward the largest city of a city system, the value of CD decreases.

8.2.3 *Spatial Convergence of Distribution of a City's Location in a Region*

Let us examine the city system from the viewpoint of the spatial convergence of the distribution of the city's location in a region. The spatial convergence (SC) of the distribution of the city's location in a region is derived by using the nearest neighbor analysis as follows. Assume that there are N_i (i = 1, 2, 3, …, N) cities in a region, of which land area is M. The distance from a city N_1 to the nearest city is denoted as d_1. This distance, d_1, is named as the least distance of the city N_1. The least distance is obtained for each of cities N_i (i = 1, 2, 3, …, N), and the average least distance (AD) between the locations of the cities in the region is derived as Eq. (8.5).

$$\mathrm{AD} = (1/N) \sum_{i=1}^{N} d_i \tag{8.5}$$

The spatial convergence of the distribution of the city's location in a region is expressed by Eq. (8.6):

$$\mathrm{SC} = \mathrm{AD}/\left(1/\left(2\,(N/M)^{0.5}\right)\right) \tag{8.6}$$

As the cities in a region locate more closely to each other, the value of SC becomes smaller. The SC's value is used to reveal the spatial characteristics of the city system in a region.

8.2.4 *Derivation of the City System Index*

Both values of CD and SC become smaller when the distribution of the city's population diverges toward the largest city and when the level of congestion of the cities' locations in region becomes higher. Hence, using these values, it is possible to construct an index that shows the structural characteristics of the city system.

This index is called the City System Index (hereafter CSI), which is derived by Eq. (8.7):

$$\mathrm{CSI} = \left((\alpha\,\mathrm{CD})^2 + (\beta\,\mathrm{SC})^2\right)^{0.5} \tag{8.7}$$

where α and β are positive parameters. When the value of the CSI is lower, it means that the structure of a city system has concentrating characteristics in terms of the city's population distribution and the locations of the cities. On the other hand, a high value of the CSI means that the structure of a city system has leveling characteristics in terms of the city's population distribution and the locations of the cities. In the rest of this chapter, CSI is used as the index that indicates the structural characteristics of the city system.

8.2.5 *City System Indexes of 47 Prefectures in Japan*

There are 47 prefectures in Japan. It may be said that a city system is found in each prefecture. Using Eq. (8.7), the CSI of each prefecture in 2008 is derived from the data of CD (the data of all cities' population in the 47 prefectures in 2008) and SC (the data of all of the cities' least distances in all prefectures in 1990; because the data of the distance is stable in the decade, the data for 1990 is used here). Table 8.1 shows the values of CD, SC, and CSI for the 47 prefectures. In the derivation of the CSI, the parameters in Eq. (8.7) are assumed to be α = 20, β = 1.

8.3 Estimation of the Social Health of 47 Prefectures in Japan

To obtain the social and economic performances of the 47 prefectures in Japan, the social health of each prefecture is estimated in terms of seven items: (a) economic base, (b) education, (c) dwelling, (d) health, (e) welfare, (f) safety, and (g) social unrest. Each of the seven items is composed of several elements, which are listed in the Appendix. The social health of each prefecture is calculated by the following procedures.

The social health of the individual prefectures is built up by the scores of the above seven items.[1] The score of an element E of an item r in a prefecture i, S_{rEi} ($r = a, b, \ldots, g$; $E = r_1, r_2, \ldots, r_n$; $i = 1, 2, 3, \ldots, 47$; r indicates item; f indicates a factor which consists r item; i shows prefecture) is derived by Eq. (8.8). The scores

[1]All data are based on "Social Indications by Prefecture," Statistics Bureau, Ministry of Internal Affairs and Communications, Japan (2011).

Table 8.1 The city system index of 47 prefectures in Japan

No.	Prefecture	CD	SC	CSI
1	Hokkaido	0.0326	1.3861	1.5325
2	Aomori	0.102	2.466875	3.201104747
3	Iwate	0.086	2.732682	3.228924089
4	Miyagi	0.054	1.986952	2.26149875
5	Akita	0.087	2.651569	3.171501253
6	Yamagata	0.089	1.587727	2.385220702
7	Fukushima	0.09	2.117017	2.778805766
8	Ibaragi	0.074	1.491258	2.10101164
9	Tochigi	0.084	1.321813	2.137659785
10	Gunma	0.101	1.750309	2.657740108
11	Saitama	0.044	1.334769	1.598751804
12	Chiba	0.051	1.867061	2.127514525
13	Tokyo	0.024	1.083915	1.185441139
14	Kanagawa	0.045	1.550007	1.792350766
15	Niigata	0.063	1.802285	2.199052707
16	Toyama	0.073	1.124717	1.842983323
17	Ishikawa	0.073	3.191603	3.509690696
18	Fukui	0.098	2.393305	3.093462571
19	Yamanashi	0.102	1.379157	2.462452632
20	Nagano	0.074	1.809893	2.337971811
21	Gifu	0.070	1.910697	2.368704956
22	Shizuoka	0.059	1.941794	2.272215385
23	Aichi	0.042	1.347925	1.588238442
24	Mie	0.084	2.141469	2.721817703
25	Shiga	0.101	1.682657	2.6290181
26	Kyoto	0.049	1.964006	2.194930513
27	Osaka	0.044	1.216331	1.501286869
28	Hyogo	0.052	2.036104	2.286332831
29	Nara	0.092	1.337015	2.274469211
30	Wakayama	0.074	4.035519	4.298350542
31	Tottori	0.135	3.504247	4.423770528
32	Shimane	0.115	3.067504	3.834003294
33	Okayama	0.066	2.496594	2.824072124
34	Hiroshima	0.053	2.334539	2.563917003
35	Yamaguchi	0.093	3.10841	3.622404374
36	Tokushima	0.103	3.631774	4.17533032
37	Kagawa	0.09	1.570651	2.38892151
38	Ehime	0.072	1.942757	2.41824425
39	Kochi	0.066	3.500824	3.74141226
40	Fukuoka	0.049	1.523937	1.811845586

(continued)

Table 8.1 (continued)

No.	Prefecture	CD	SC	CSI
41	Saga	0.115	2.40255	3.325995321
42	Nagasaki	0.076	2.456682	2.88889017
43	Kumamoto	0.051	2.733707	2.917799644
44	Oita	0.067	2.895773	3.190784083
45	Miyazaki	0.089	2.916389	3.41668373
46	Kagoshima	0.055	2.651677	2.870782209
47	Okinawa	0.093	1.412201	2.335361019

of the seven items and the social health of the 47 prefectures are indicated in Table 8.2.

$$S_{rEi} = (X_{rEi} - AV_{rE})/\mathrm{ST}_{rE} \quad (r = a, b, \ldots, g;\ \ E = r_1, r_2, \ldots, r_n;\ \ i = 1, 2, \ldots, 47) \tag{8.8}$$

where X_{rEi} is a datum value of the element E in the r item in the prefecture i. AV_{rE} is the mean value of the element E in the r item; ST_{rE} is the standard deviation of the element E of the r item.

The score of the r item of a prefecture i (i = 1, 2, …, 47) is obtained by Eq. (8.9):

$$S_{ri} = (1/n) \sum_{E=r_1}^{r_n} S_{rEi} \quad (r = a, b, \ldots, g;\ \ i = 1, 2, \ldots, 47) \tag{8.9}$$

The social health (SH) of a prefecture i is made up by the scores of the seven items; the value of the social health by obtained by Eq. (8.10):

$$\mathrm{SH}_i = (1/7) \sum_{r=a}^{g} S_{ri} \quad (i = 1, 2, \ldots, 47) \tag{8.10}$$

Table 8.2 Scores of items and social health of 47 prefectures in Japan

Prefecture	Economic base	Education	Dwelling	Health	Welfare	Safety	Social unrest	Social health
Hokkaido	−0.5341	0.605482	0.31498	0.72302	0.4272	0.1203	0.12035	0.1579369
Aomori	−0.8877	0.196016	0.06229	−0.1804	0.7302	−0.089	−0.0888	−0.015901
Iwate	−0.7406	0.267378	−0.161	−0.1082	−0.262	0.3738	0.37377	−0.076508
Miyagi	−0.2392	0.245402	−0.0015	−0.6085	−0.801	0.0047	0.00469	−0.201974
Akita	−0.5714	0.281897	0.50981	0.12453	0.6935	0.4936	0.4936	0.2617918
Yamagata	−0.455	0.297927	0.24969	−0.4101	−0.293	−0.017	−0.0167	−0.05266
Fukushima	−0.2929	−0.19249	0.00988	−0.1889	−0.677	0.6778	0.67781	−0.078809
Ibaragi	0.50222	−0.20327	−0.4303	−0.7005	−1.037	−0.335	−0.335	−0.388862
Tochigi	0.31497	−0.19294	−0.1242	−0.4792	−1.239	−0.77	−0.77	−0.365233
Gunma	0.4072	−0.34228	0.04396	−0.3666	−0.613	−0.288	−0.2879	−0.213944
Saitama	0.5766	−0.29667	−0.5955	−1.2893	−1.639	−0.314	−0.3144	−0.536352
Chiba	0.85972	0.074178	−0.5741	−0.9258	−1.625	0.0641	0.06412	−0.326373
Tokyo	1.50449	0.756757	−0.4638	0.4346	−0.012	−0.243	−0.2428	0.2891645
Kanagawa	0.80846	0.103219	−0.7603	−1.0246	−1.204	−0.409	−0.4086	−0.376051
Niigata	−0.0259	−0.07173	0.39697	−0.2715	−0.371	0.5362	0.53619	0.0542602
Toyama	0.2631	−0.30194	0.35522	0.01069	−0.257	0.9618	0.96178	0.1577868
Ishikawa	−0.0456	0.124381	0.42154	0.02255	−0.083	0.9698	0.9698	0.230044
Fukui	0.06327	−0.2663	0.52452	−0.2638	0.1974	0.2964	0.29641	0.1302644
Yamanashi	0.0038	0.188246	0.15172	−0.0744	0.2209	−0.569	−0.5692	0.035173
Nagano	0.23445	−0.44702	0.50994	−0.3053	−0.211	−0.284	−0.2844	−0.048605
Gifu	0.36025	−0.43951	0.32432	−0.639	−0.833	0.0646	0.06465	−0.178033
Shizuoka	0.77199	−0.79904	−0.0981	−0.9237	−1.347	−0.092	−0.0923	−0.407769
Aichi	1.69099	−0.24711	−0.2891	−1.011	−1.126	−0.309	−0.3086	−0.314072
Mie	0.58228	−0.29559	−0.2121	−0.5225	−0.619	−0.12	−0.12	−0.189973

(continued)

Table 8.2 (continued)

Prefecture	Economic base	Education	Dwelling	Health	Welfare	Safety	Social unrest	Social health
Shiga	0.46197	0.066235	−0.1519	−0.9748	−0.782	0.0064	0.0064	−0.185594
Kyoto	0.3627	0.904434	0.0815	0.11052	0.0994	0.131	0.13096	0.283651
Osaka	0.30552	−0.22915	−0.3621	−0.0504	−0.088	−1.071	−1.0715	−0.275277
Hyogo	0.44302	−0.0332	0.00952	−0.5288	−0.504	0.2618	0.26184	−0.156139
Nara	0.04017	0.21935	0.09594	−0.3287	−0.529	−0.009	−0.009	−0.024406
Wakayama	−0.3718	−0.31203	−0.1105	0.53286	0.674	−0.698	−0.6979	−0.024257
Tottori	−0.4786	0.33481	0.42856	0.34943	1.3939	0.1993	0.19928	0.4016482
Shimane	−0.4159	0.680282	0.45458	0.7841	1.0957	0.4627	0.46272	0.5268948
Okayama	0.11259	0.084917	−0.0626	0.35207	−0.104	0.1141	0.11409	−0.01962
Hiroshima	0.38273	−0.07315	0.02329	0.19995	−0.084	0.1229	0.12291	0.0528726
Yamaguchi	0.14424	0.114507	0.15113	0.46324	0.4454	0.0069	0.00688	0.2411563
Tokushima	−0.4146	0.235505	−0.2051	1.0854	0.9501	0.5026	0.5026	0.350007
Kagawa	0.09688	−0.31289	0.08268	0.18689	0.2383	0.1731	0.17307	−0.001101
Ehime	−0.2755	−0.07951	−0.2304	0.33731	0.4307	−0.101	−0.1011	−0.012447
Kochi	−0.8023	0.241263	0.23549	1.58716	1.5612	−0.404	−0.4036	0.3152828
Fukuoka	−0.0187	−0.17413	−0.404	0.69839	0.3575	−0.738	−0.7377	−0.13451
Saga	−0.4282	−0.29224	−0.0003	0.71007	0.5886	0.2593	0.25929	0.1526213
Nagasaki	−0.8333	−0.12967	−0.1046	1.00878	1.2978	0.3388	0.33875	0.2923275
Kumamoto	−0.5389	0.12158	−0.2791	0.70208	0.5587	0.4606	0.46062	0.1951235
Oita	−0.4568	0.044558	−0.0569	0.37063	0.8741	−0.069	−0.0694	0.1072699
Miyazaki	−0.4844	−0.29376	0.36561	0.31078	0.9605	−0.337	−0.3369	0.0922719
Kagoshima	−0.8272	0.292688	−0.0097	1.07491	1.3794	0.191	0.19104	0.3265861
Okinawa	−1.481	−0.62855	−0.137	−0.0668	0.8263	−0.347	−0.3474	−0.156854

8.4 Relationships Between the City System and a Prefecture's Performances

8.4.1 Relationship Between City Systems and Economic Performance of Regions

First, let us examine the relationship between the CSIs and the scores for the economic base of the 47 prefectures in Japan. As shown in Fig. 8.1, there is a clear relationship between the structures of the city systems in prefectures and the economic performances achieved in the prefectures. As the city system has concentrating characteristics in terms of population distribution and location of the cities, its economic performance tends to be higher.

8.4.2 The Relationship Between City Systems and Welfare of Regions

Second, let us examine the relationship between the CSIs and the scores for the welfare of the prefectures in Japan. As shown in Fig. 8.2, there is a clear

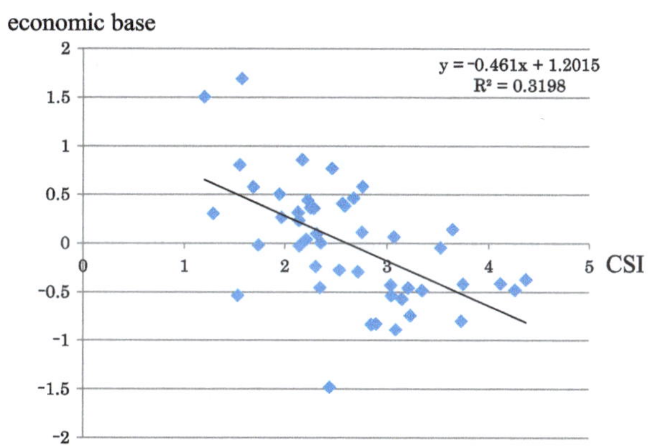

Fig. 8.1 Relationship between CSI and economic performance of prefectures

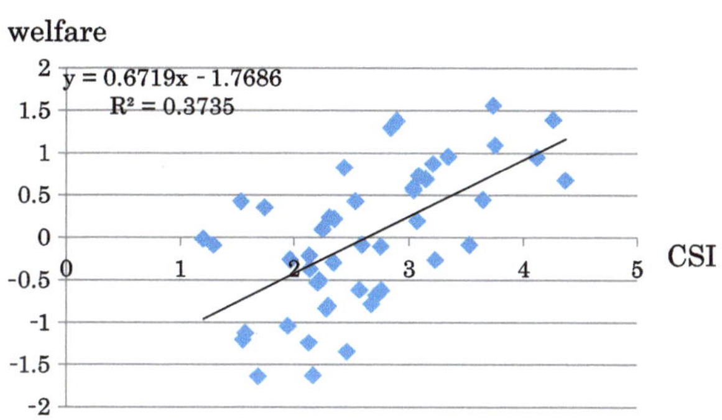

Fig. 8.2 Relationship between CSIs and welfare of prefectures

relationship between the structure of the city systems in prefectures and the social performances achieved in the prefectures. As the structure of the city system in a prefecture has leveling characteristics, the prefecture's welfare performance tends to be higher.

8.4.3 No Relationship Between City Systems and the Education of Regions

The relationship between the CSIs and the scores for education of the prefectures in Japan is shown in Fig. 8.3. There is not a clear relationship between the CSIs and the scores for education of the prefectures.

8.4.4 Relationship Between City Systems and Social Health of Regions

Of the seven relationships between the CSIs and an item composing the social health, the three relationships that represent the typical trends are selected; they are shown in the above three figures, Figs. 8.1, 8.2 and 8.3. Of the seven relationships, six relationships display almost the same trend: as the CSI increases, the score of each item becomes relatively higher. Only one item for economic performance displays the opposite trend: as the CSI increases, its score becomes lower.

Then, let us examine the relationship between the CSIs and social health, which consists of seven items. Figure 8.4 shows the relationship. As the structure of the city system has leveling characteristics in terms of the population distribution and the location of the cities, the social health of a region tends to be higher.

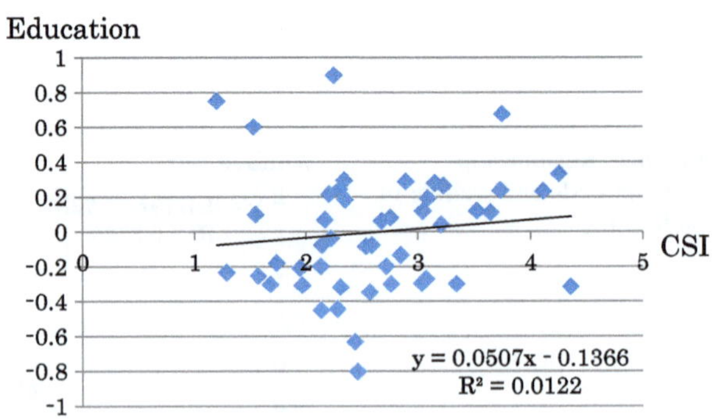

Fig. 8.3 Relationship between CSIs and education of prefectures

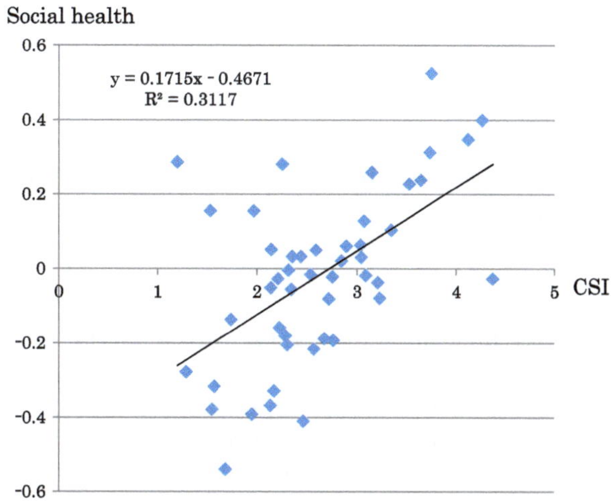

Fig. 8.4 Relationship between CSIs and social health of prefecture

8.5 City System as a Location Factor

Based on the results of above analyses, it could be said that if some firms make much of the production efficiency of the factory, they should select a city system that has converging characteristics. If other firms consider the region's welfare level as the most important factor in the selection of a region, they should select a city system that has leveling characteristics. This selection may be reasonable if a firm's factory produces knowledge-incentive products by using many workers with high technology. When firms must equally pay attention to both the production efficiency of a new factory and the level of the welfare of a region, they may choose a city system for which the CSI is average range of values of the CSI.[2]

When a manufacturing firm has a project to build a new factory, the determination of the factory's location is the most important in the project. Because a firm does not have enough information on the economic and the social conditions of all potential location areas and sites, the manufacturer cannot determine its location site immediately. A series of steps are taken to decide the final location. A firm narrows the range of the search area step by step toward the final determination. In the first half of the determination processes, two steps are taken: (1) set the LPA as a large geographical area, which is examined in part 2; and (2) select a potential region within the LPA. In the first step, a chaotic phenomenon may be useful to identify a prospective area. In the second step, in the selection of a potential region for a factory's location, the city systems in the region play an important role. Because the city system in a region reveals the economic and social performances achieved in

[2]Ishikawa-Wall (2015) use the same index, CSI and show the relationships between the CSI and regions' performances in regions in Japan and Sweden.

the region, the city system is clearly a location factor in the decision-making processes of a firm's region selection.

Appendix: Elements of the Seven Items Composing Social Health

(a) Economic base:

1. Prefectural income per person, \1000.
2. Value of manufactured goods shipments, etc., \100 million.
3*. Unemployment rate, both sexes.
4*. Regional difference index of consumer prices, Tokyo = 100.
5. Index of financial potential, prefecture.
6. Starting salary, senior high school graduates, month, male and female, \1000.
7. Salary of part-time worker, hour, female, \1.

(b) Education:

8. Elementary school pupil, per teacher.
9. Exercise ground area of pupil, elementary schools, per pupil, m^2.
10. Entrance capacity index of colleges and universities.
11. Ratio of people having completed up to colleges and universities, %.

(c) Dwelling:

12. Ratio of owned houses, %.
13. Dwelling rooms, per dwelling,
14*. Monthly rent, owned by private corporation, per m^2, \1000.
15. Ratio of households covered by city gas supply system,%.
16. Diffusion rate of sewerage, %.
17. Ratio of forest area, %.
18. Area of public parks per capita, m^2.
19. Ratio of major roads paved, %.
20. Retail stores excluding eating and drinking places etc., per 1000 persons.
21. Eating and drinking places, per 1000 persons.
22. Sports facilities, per 1,000,000 persons.

(d) Health:

23. Physicians working at medical establishments, per 100,000 persons.
24. Beds in general hospitals, per 100,000 persons.
25. Dental clinics, per 100,000 persons.
26. Beds for mental diseases, per 100,000 persons.
27. Ambulances clinics, per 100,000 persons.

(e) Welfare:

28. Homes for the aged, per 100,000 persons, 65 years old and over.
29. Rehabilitation facilities for physically disabled persons, per 1,000,000 persons.
30. Child welfare institutions, per 100,000 persons.
31. Welfare expenditure per capita, prefecture + municipality, \1000.
32. Social welfare expenditure per capita, prefecture + municipality, \1000.
33. Social welfare expenditure for aged person per capita 65 years old and over, prefecture + municipality, \1000.

(f) Safety:

34*. Traffic accidents, per 100,000 persons.
35*. Persons killed or injured by fires, per 100,000 persons.
36. Fire engines and cars existing, per 100,000 persons.
37. Police men, per1000 persons.
38*. Recognitions of criminal offences, per 1000 persons.
39*. Death by accidents, per 100,000 persons.
40*. Soot and smoke emitting facilities.
41*. General dust discharging facilities.

(g) Social unrest:

42*. Cases indicted for drug law, per 100,000 persons.
43*. Cases of grievance against pollution, per 100,000 persons.
44*. Rate of divorces, per 1000 persons, %.
45*. Suicides, per 100,000 persons.
46*. Ration of long-term absences from junior high school students due to refusal to attend school 30 days and more for a school year, per 1000 students.

(The mark "*" denotes that the element of which value is lower, its score becomes higher.)

References

Arndt, S. W., & Kierzkowski, H. (2001). *Fragmentation*. Oxford: Oxford University Press.

Baumol, W. J., & Ide, E. A. (1956). Variety in retailing. *Management Science, 3*, 93–101.

Beckmann, M. J., & McPherson, J. C. (1970). City size distribution in a central place Hierarchy: An alternative approach. *Journal of Regional Science, 10*(1), 25–33.

Capello, R. (2004). Beyond optimal city size: Theory and evidence reconsidered. In R. Capello & R. Nijkamp (Eds.), *Urban dynamics and growth*. Amsterdam: Elsevier.

Capello, R. (2007). *Regional economics* (pp. 203–205). London: Routledge.

Capozza, D., & Van Order, R. (1978). A generalized model of spatial competition. *American Economic Review, 68*, 896–908.

Christaller, W. (1933). *Die Zentralen Orte in Süddeutschland*. Jena: Gustav Fisher.

Dluhosch, B. (2000). *Industrial location and economic integration—Centrifugal and centripetal forces in the New Europe*. Cheltenham: Edgar Elgar.

Eden, L. (1985). The microeconomics of transfer pricing. In M. Rugman & L. Eden (Eds.), *Multinationals and transfer pricing*. New York: St. Martin's Press.

Greenhut, M. L. (1956). *Plant location in theory and in practice*. Chapel Hill: University of North Carolina Press.

Greenhut, M. L., & Ohta, H. (1973). Spatial configurations and competitive equilibrium. *Weltwirtschaftliches Archive*, Bd. 109, SS. 87–104.

Hirshleifer, J. (1956, July). On the economics of transfer pricing. *Journal of Business, 29*(3), 172–184.

Hoover, E. M. (1937). *Location* ***theory and the shoe and leather industries***. New York: Harvard University Press.

Hoover, E. M. (1970). Transport cost and the spacing of central places. *Papers of Regional Science Association, 25*, 255–274.

Hotelling, H. (1929). Stability in competition. *Economic Journal, 39*, 41–57.

Ishikawa, T. (2009). Determination of a factory's location in a large Geographical area by using chaotic phenomena and retailers' location networks. *Timisoara Journal of Economics, 2*, 141–150.

Ishikawa, T. (2015a). Fragmentation of production process due to growth and survival competition. In T. Ishikawa (Ed.), *Firms' location selections and regional policy in the global economy*. Springer: Tokyo.

Ishikawa, T. (2015b). Effects of corporation tax rates on factory locations through the function of the transfer price. In T. Ishikawa (Ed.), *Firms' location selections and regional policy in the global economy*. Springer: Tokyo.

Ishikawa, T., & Toda, M. (1990). Spatial configurations, competition and welfare. *Annals of Regional Science, 24*, 1–12.

Ishikawa, T., & Toda, M. (1995). An unequal spatial structure of location and price with consumer density. *Economic Record, 71*, 167–178.

T. Ishikawa, *Dynamic Locational Phases of Economic Activity in the Globalized World*, DOI 10.1007/978-981-10-0524-4

Ishikawa, T., & Toda, M. (1998). An Application of the frontier price concept in spatial equilibrium analysis. *Urban Studies, 35*(8), 1345–1358.

Ishikawa, T., & Toda, M. (2000). Some economic extensions of central-place theory involving profit maximisation. *Urban Studies, 37*, 481–495.

Ishikawa, T., & Toda, M. (2002). On the optimal locational policy for the offshore firm entering a foreign market area. *Canadian Journal of regional science, XXV*(3), 353–376.

Ishikawa, T., & Wall, R. (2015). Significance of constructing city systems in regional policy. T. Ishikawa (Ed.), *Firms' location selections and regional policy in the global economy*. Springer: Tokyo.

Keizai, T. (2002). *Chiikikeizai Soran* (Data Book, in Japanese). Tokyo.

Kozu, H. (1998). Industrial agglomeration in city centers. *Journal of Managerial Research, 71*, 1–14. Institute of Managerial Research, Aichi University.

Lazonick, A. (1986). The cotton industry. In B. Elbaum & W. Lazonick (Eds.), *The decline of the British economy* (pp. 18–50). Oxford: Oxford University Press.

Lerner, A. P., & Singer, H. W. (1937). Some notes on duopoly and spatial competition. *Journal of Political Economy, XLV*, 145–186.

Lösch, A. (1940). *Die räumliche Ordnung der Wirtschaft*. Jena: Gustav Fischer.

Miyasaka, M. (1970). *Location theory of manufacturing industry*. Tokyo (in Japanese): Kokonshoin.

Parr, J. B. (1978). Models of the central-place system: A more generalized approach. *Urban Studies, 15*, 35–49.

Parr, J. B. (1988). Income, trade and the balance of payments within an urban system. *Journal of Regional Science, 28*, 1–14.

Parr, J. B. (1995). The economic law of market areas: A further discussion. *Journal of Regional Science, 35*, 599–615.

Puu, T. (1998). Gradient dynamics in Weberian location theory. In M. J. Beckmann et al. (Eds.), *Knowledge and networks in a dynamic economy* (Vol. 34, pp. 569–589). Berlin: Springer.

Romer, P. (1990, October). Endogenous technological change. *Journal of Political Economy*, 98, S71–S102.

Sakashita, N. (1967). *Production function, demand function and location theory of the firm* (pp. 423–428). XX: Papers of Regional Science Association.

Sassen, S. (1991). *The global city: New York, London, Tokyo*. Princeton: Princeton University Press.

Schöler, K. (1993). Consistent conjectural variations in a two-dimensional spatial market. *Regional Science and Urban Economics, 23*, 765–778.

Sheppard, E. (1982). City size distributions and spatial economic change. *International Regional Science Review, 7*(2), 127–151.

Shi, H., & Yang, X. (1995). A new theory of industrialization. *Journal of Comparative Economics, 20*, 171–189.

Smithies, A. (1941). Optimal location in spatial competition. *Journal of Political Economy, 49*, 423–439.

Statistics Bureau, Ministry of internal affairs and communications, Japan. (2011). *Social indications by prefecture 2011*. Statistics Sweden, http://www.scb.se

Suh, S. E. (1991). The optimal size distribution size distribution of cities. *Journal of Urban Economics, 30*, 182–192.

Tinbergen, J. (1968). The hierarchy model of the size distribution of centres. *Papers of the Regional Science Association, 20*, 65–68.

Weber, A. (1909). *Über den Standort der Industrien*. Tubingen: J.C.B. Mohr.

Zipf, G. K. (1941). *National unity and distribution*. Bloomington: Principia Press.

MIX
Papier aus verantwortungsvollen Quellen
Paper from responsible sources
FSC® C105338

If you have any concerns about our products,
you can contact us on
ProductSafety@springernature.com

In case Publisher is established outside the EU,
the EU authorized representative is:
Springer Nature Customer Service Center GmbH
Europaplatz 3, 69115 Heidelberg, Germany

Printed by Libri Plureos GmbH
in Hamburg, Germany